THE BOOK OF DIP:
HOW GOD CAN CHANGE A MAN, A MARRIAGE, AND MORE

by

FLOYD "DIPPER" GARRISON

Table of Contents

Foreword by Franklin Graham
Author's Introduction

Foreword

If you want to read a one-of-a-kind story, *The Book of Dip* is a good pick. Not many New Jersey boys could transplant to Boone, NC, and make a mark like Dipper did many years ago. His love for the High Country is evidenced in his personal account, but more than that is his love for people from all walks of life. He is a man who seeks opportunity for the Gospel, and barrels through every open door. His journey has been full of trials and triumphs, spattered with motorcycle- and car wrecks, injuries, and near-death experiences. Through it all, he has lived to tell how a broken life can be stitched together by the miraculous and intervening hand of the miracle-working God of Heaven.

Whether negotiating a business deal or building personal friendships, Dipper is driven to testify about what the Lord Jesus will do for anyone who will repent and receive Christ as personal Savior. While Dipper is nicknamed for his incredible ability to "dip" a basketball into the net, Floyd Garrison's real story is that he dipped his heart into the saving blood of Jesus Christ. His outspoken testimony for what God has done with a life that started out difficult will tenderize hardened hearts and lead them to the One who is "clothed in a robe *dipped* in blood, and His name is called the Word of God" (Revelation 19:13). Every life matters to Him!

Franklin Graham
President & CEO
Samaritan's Purse
Billy Graham Evangelistic Association

Author's Introduction

Do you believe in God, and that He does miracles?

If not, maybe you will after reading the story of my life! If you *do* already believe, may my story encourage you and bring God the glory, because He's the *only* reason I'm alive to write this book. God put it best, in Jeremiah 29:11: *For I know the plans I have for you, says the Lord; plans for welfare and not for evil, to give you a future and a hope.*

Amen to *that*!

My story is recounted to the best of my ability, and is as close to the facts as I can remember (for things that happened over 70 years ago). It is not fiction, but the true account of what can happen because of the prayers of a loving, Godly mother, and others who intervened so that I could have an abundant life, for which I'm eternally grateful. My prayer is that my story will affect many people and show how God clearly moves in a person's life—even yours!

On that note: if anything in this book sounds like I'm boasting or bragging, I pray you'll understand that my story is all about the Lord and what He did, not my accomplishments. In that respect, I'm like Paul Anderson: unable to pick up a penny without God's help.

And, before we begin, a word of wisdom: always remember that "coincidence" is spelled "G-O-D."

Now, enjoy God's story, for he's really the One who wrote this book. Give Him all the praise and glory!

Chapter I: The Beginning

It's January 1st, 2015, and I'm in my house in Boone, NC, up in the Appalachian mountains. It's snowing outside, and I'm keeping a promise I made to myself and to God: that I would write my autobiography, the "Book of Dip." It has been on my bucket list of things to do, and I've been trying to write it for the past five years. But, as usual, I hadn't been able to slow down enough to do it, despite it being a really big part of my life. (I just recently got caught up on my mail, after being two years behind.) It seems I've been going full throttle, non-stop, my whole life.

And oh! what a life it's been. Hold on tight, and let me tell you a story!

* * *

It all began on November 24th, 1944, in Bridgeton, NJ (that's south Jersey, below the Mason-Dixon line—I'm a southern boy). I was born Floyd Horace Garrison. "Floyd" came from my mother's brother, who died at one year of age. "Horace" referred to my father, Horace Garrison (a name which I always thought to be funny and ironic, since my dad's favorite things were playing cards and going to the race track—"race" and "ace" plus "Horace" sounds like "horse"). He didn't like his name, and everyone called him Gary. I don't like mine, either.

Because my dad was a sergeant in the Army, serving overseas in World War II, I didn't see him for the first part of my life. That's probably why I was a mama's boy until I was eleven years old (more on this later). Until she married Dad, my mother's name was Pearl Taylor. Having grown up on a farm, she was a real tomboy, and, standing 6'1" and weighing about 140 pounds, she looked the part. Yet she was pretty, and funny. She loved music, able to play the guitar and other string instruments. She could shoot a gun like Annie Oakley. She played sports, cooked and baked unbelievably, loved animals, and attended a Methodist church. She loved my dad with all her heart, and she loved the Lord, too—a sweet, Godly woman. I never heard my mom or dad argue, or so much as exchange an unkind word; I only remember them laughing and loving up on one another. My dad was a good man who kept his word and worked hard, and would never lie, cheat, or steal; but, unlike his wife, he didn't know the Lord. He loved my mother with all his heart (she was his everything!), but she was the *only* person he knew how to love, probably from having been born as the last of eighteen children.

We lived in a little area called Center Grove, five miles from Millville, NJ. We had a nice little home there, situated between my maternal grandfather's place and that of my mom's sister (my Aunt Beulah), who lived with her husband, Aim. Center Grove was where I first encountered how God works, through something that happened when I was a young child.

I had some breathing problems at the time, and these would be responsible for the incident in question (which, as it turned out, was the first of many near-death experiences in my life). Our house stood alone, a ways from anyone else, and my dad was still overseas; so it was only me and my mom, and she didn't have a car at the time, further isolating us. It was night out, and I was in the kitchen when I suddenly stopped breathing and turned blue. All my mom could do is pray. Just at that moment, my Uncle Aim was on his way home from work, which sent him by our house. Right as he went by, he had the oddest thought: that he should stop by and check on us! As Aim came through the kitchen door and saw me on the floor, he ran over and resuscitated me, getting me breathing again.

Had he not stopped, I wouldn't be here. God answered my mother's prayer that night (and not for the last time).

Later that same year, another big thing happened: Horace "Gary" Garrison returned home. At last, I got to meet my father.

Yet, meet him was about all I did. He began working immediately after his discharge from the service, and he left early and got home late. When he wasn't working, he did what he enjoyed: going to the American Legion; playing poker; spending Saturdays at the race track. We didn't have a lot of time together; I don't think he knew how to be a father. It didn't help that I'd become a mama's boy during his three years away! My mother kept encouraging him to be involved with me, so when I was around seven he started taking me hunting at his parents' farm. This was good because some of the best times I ever had with my dad was during our hunting excursions!

I must tell you about my paternal grandparents. Grandpa was around sixty when my dad was born, and Grandma was in her fifties; as I mentioned earlier, my dad was the last of eighteen kids (only sixteen lived, with two dying at birth). Pa was about 5'6" and weighed 115 pounds, while Ma was 6'1" and close to *200* pounds. Their farm, where my dad took me hunting, had chickens, pigeons, cows, and pigs. I can still remember Pa in his rocker on the front porch, with his corncob pipe. Ma got up every day at 4:30 AM to start cooking breakfast for the family—she did everything! If Pa requested more firewood, Ma would pick up the ax and throw on her cape, and out the back door she'd go. Or, she'd go out and pump some water, or tend to the chickens (Pa was in charge of the other livestock, and the pigeons). What a woman she was! When I saw the movie *Ma and Pa Kettle*, I thought it was about them. The only difference was that they didn't have an Indian living with them.

Ma and Pa Garrison lived long and were great parents. My dad and I continued hunting and fishing at their farm for several years.

* * *

Other than that, there's not much to say about my early childhood. Growing up, I went to school and worked—the one consistent thing in my life, work. It began when I was five, in my neighbor's strawberry patch, where I started picking at five cents a quart. I'd pick berries all day long, which led to a strawberry stand when I was six. I sold lots of berries, plus I started selling newspapers and working in the fields of other farmers. I liked making money.

One farmer lived six miles away. When I was around ten, I'd walk and hitchhike to his farm. Though a Christian, he was a tough man to work for. At fifty cents an hour, he didn't have much compassion for me—and the work was *hard*. I can still remember being out in the field in hundred-degree weather, with flies and mosquitoes as big as bees. The farmer's wife would bring out iced tea—so cold, and it tasted so great! Too bad the deal wasn't as good as it appeared, for her husband charged twenty-five cents a glass (which I didn't know until I first got paid, at the end of the week). I had some hard feelings toward him, but there *was* one good thing that came from that job: at the end of the summer of 1956, he asked if I would go to Philadelphia, PA, to attend a Billy Graham crusade with his family. I had never been out of Jersey, and I couldn't wait to go, even though I didn't know who Billy Graham was! I had gone to church with my mom, but I don't remember hearing the gospel message until that night in Philly. It was, I believe, like God planted a seed in me then. I'll never forget seeing all those people going forth, and I'll always be grateful to that farmer, even if he was a hard man who charged me a quarter for a drink of tea!

Soon after that, I turned eleven, and experienced a life-changing event—*two* of them, actually.

The first was when I got a little brother named Raymon. I tell people to this day: though born ten years apart, Raymon and I are twins! It's how alike we are. I don't think my parents planned for him, but oh! how my mother loved Raymon. Soon afterward, however, that second big change arrived. Everything seemed fine for the first six months after Raymon's birth, but then my mother began having a hard time. She seemed different, suddenly not herself. It was then, for the first time ever, she lost her patience with me over some small thing. I didn't understand what was going on—and then they were taking my mother away to a hospital! All I was told was that she had some problem and would be gone for a while.

Afterward, I could tell my dad wasn't right. He never seemed happy to me; in reality, he was very depressed. But no one told me what was going on, so it was a great shock when, about five months later, I got off the school bus one afternoon to find all these cars parked around my house. I knew something was strange, and when I got to the door, I was met with explosive news: my mother had died. I can't remember who told me. All I remember is running to a tree in our yard, throwing my arms around it, and crying. I clung to that tree for what seemed like eternity. My dad never said anything until after the funeral. I guess he was in shock like me.

I can still remember the pain. Apparently, my mom, dad, and other family members had thought it best to keep quiet about things. Right or wrong, I regret the decision, because I never got a chance to tell my wonderful, loving mother goodbye and how much I loved her. I hated having lost those five months of seeing her, and the precious time we could've had together. I was told later, in 1956, that the reason they didn't want me to see her or know about the cancer was because they really couldn't help her. She was in great pain (for which she received only aspirin), and she went from 140 pounds to 86. I remember how much different she looked when I saw her at the funeral, which was one of the worst and hardest days of memory.

At the time, I didn't realize how my mother's death was going to impact the rest of my life. The change became apparent on the day of the funeral, when we got home from the burial and everyone had left. My dad came over to the chair I was sitting in, looked down at me, and said these words: "Son, I just as well might've been in that casket with your mother, because I'm a dead man! The only thing I promise you is I'll try to keep a roof over your head. But other than that, you're on your own!"

Wow! Here's this little eleven-year-old kid who's just lost the most important person on this earth (and is a mama's boy, no less), and I'm suddenly "on my own"! *Life change* doesn't cover it! My dad wasn't exaggerating, either, because we faced some hard times then. First, he had to sell our wonderful home and move us into a trailer, for he needed to hire a live-in caretaker for little Raymon and me, but couldn't afford both that and the house. Second, my dad himself changed. For the next several years he was like a zombie. He went to work; he played cards; he went to bed. And that was it. Raymon was more like a son than a little brother, and my life was turned completely on its head. The only good thing that came of it was that, after a few housekeepers who didn't really care, my dad hired Mrs. Cox, an older woman who didn't have much strength left but was a good

4

person and showed real concern for all of us! She stayed on for several years.

One other good thing came of these sweeping changes in my life: they instilled in me the driven personality that I possess to this day. Other than the food and housing my dad provided, it fell on me to supply anything else I might need. From then on, I developed a strong work ethic, and it would only escalate. Lemons really can be made into lemonade, I suppose.

Despite all the pain and upset of my mother's death, life did go on. Our little family pulled through, and we didn't starve. My dad did finally come back to life, after which he would eventually remarry. The woman's name was Eleanor, and she took good care of Dad and Raymon—another godsend! As for me, my life began a whole new chapter.

Chapter II: After Losing My Mother

Things kept changing in the wake of my mother's death.

I had lost my mom, and all her love was gone. I went from being a good, cheerful mama's boy who felt secure and loved, to a confused and lonely twelve-year-old who was mad at God for taking his mother (and was "on his own" to boot). The result was a rebellious kid going down a dark, dead-end road to nowhere. The only bright spot was my mother's sister, my Aunt Beulah from down the road, who loved on me and tried to help me. But my heart had been broken and hardened, and I was no longer little "Floydy Boy."

By then I was approaching thirteen, had hit puberty, and had begun to develop the outsize body I would possess as a man. I was already six feet tall, wearing a size-thirteen shoe and looking nothing like my age. Accordingly, I was starting to run around with older kids who weren't nice little boys. But things weren't all bad. During this time, I developed an interest in a game called basketball, so that when I hit fourteen and entered high school (and was well over six feet, with a fourteen shoe), I was off to the races. I tried out for the team, and made it.

I liked playing basketball (and, the attention it brought from girls!). Toward the end of that first season, I was beginning to dunk the ball, and that's how I got my original nickname, "Dunker," though this soon changed. We had a big game one Friday night, and the cheerleaders came to me and said, "We have some new cheers for you, but they don't go with 'Dunker.'" I asked, "What do they go with, then?" and they answered, "Dipper." I said, "That's fine!"

That night, I scored twenty-eight points, and the next day my picture was in the paper with the headline "Dipper Scores 28 Points—Big Win For Millville High." I've been called Dipper ever since. (Sure beats Floyd.)

Soon after that landmark game, I had my second near-death experience.

This time, instead of nearly suffocating on a kitchen floor, it was an infection that threatened my life. I had strep to begin with, and then, while playing a basketball game on an outdoor court, I fell and scraped up my leg. I didn't think anything about it at the time, but within a couple days I didn't feel good at all. Little did I know what I was in for, and that it would be another crucial moment in my life.

I went to a doctor, and the next thing I knew, I was in the hospital with a fever of 107. Before the day was over, I was in a coma. As it turned out, the infection in my throat had combined with that in my leg, forming a super-bug of sorts, which the doctors couldn't stop. It was going to kill me, they said. My family was brought to the hospital, and as I was lying there, still comatose, I heard them being told to say their goodbyes because I wasn't going to make it through the night! So there I was, only fourteen and thinking I wouldn't see another sunrise. I felt fine, except I just couldn't wake up or move, or respond to what was happening around me. What was going on here? Well, a miracle, that's what.

My cure came in the form of a mysterious package, like something out of a movie. At midnight that night, when the nurse on my floor went to the nurses' station, she saw a box lying there. All it said was "for infection," nothing else. The nurse called the doctor and asked if he had ordered something for me. He said he hadn't, but to go ahead and administer the stuff, because I was going to die anyway. So she did.

That was a Monday night (in 1959), and by Friday, I felt so good that I got up, dressed, and ran ten blocks to the high school—we had a basketball game, and I didn't want to miss it! I arrived just as the bus was leaving with the team. When I knocked on the side, the bus stopped and the coach threw the door open. "Dipper, what are you doing here?" he said. "You're supposed to be *dead*!" I answered, "No, I feel great, and I'm ready to play ball." The coach grinned and told me to get on, and away we went! The only problem was, I'd forgotten to tell the hospital I was leaving. They discovered me missing, and went searching the grounds. Meanwhile, one of the older nurses was a basketball fan and had the game on the radio, and she soon shouted, "I know where he's at!" I had just scored two points, and the next thing I knew, there was a gurney and two medics putting me on it, to return me to the hospital.

See God's hand in all this? Remember, I had a praying mother!

* * *

I did recover fully from that super-infection, but my troubles were far from over.

My education, for one. The classes I took in high school were not preparing me for college. Nobody in the Garrison family had ever gone beyond high school; from the way things were looking, I would be no different. Instead of higher learning, I pursued shop classes, basketball, girls, work, and fun! After basketball season I got a fulltime job catching

8

chickens. (Yes, someone has to catch them and put them in the crates you see on the back of trailers going to market.) It was a good job, though the money enabled me in less-than-healthy ways. I was still hanging out with an older crowd, except now going to bars and chasing women! At sixteen, I was still in high school, but at 6'6" with a size-sixteen shoe, I didn't look like any high-school kid. Basketball was going well, and I liked the shop classes, but I was a bit of a mess. Thankfully, two things happened that year.

First, I was influenced by my social studies teacher, a good man who seemed to care about me. During one of his classes, he made a profound statement that really changed my direction in life. Basically, he explained that it doesn't hurt to have dreams for your future, for if you're willing to work hard and stay focused, dreams can come true and nothing is impossible. Before that, I'd never really thought about life after high school, or what I was going to do or what I would be, so my teacher's advice was a real eye-opener. For the first time, I started thinking about the future and dreaming about a life to come—wow!

The second thing that happened that year: my next job. On the way home from basketball practice one day, I noticed a sign in the window of a hardware store: "HELP WANTED." I was tired of chasing chickens, so I walked in and met the store's owner, Jack Howell of Howell's Hardware. Mr. Howell was about 5'8", and everything in the store went up ten-foot-high shelve walls. When I asked for the job, he looked between me, standing over six-and-a-half feet, and the ladder used for reaching the inventory. A big grin opened on his face. "You're hired," he said, sounding pleased. He wouldn't need the ladder anymore.

Jack Howell was a blessing to me for many years, for he became the father figure I lost when my mother passed. Right from the start, he was very kind. Jack supported me both financially and emotionally, and encouraged me every day through my two remaining years of high school (and even into college; more on this in the next chapter). The hardware store was more than a job, serving as an education in itself. I learned so much that would help me later on in life, both in building and in business. And Jack really did care, as did his wife, Betty. The Howells never knew how much they meant to me, just like Mrs. Cox and my Aunt Beulah, unaware of how much I appreciated all that they did! It was regrettable; but then, there's so much we never know in this regard. Whether these people knew of my gratitude or not, I'm just glad they were there for me, to change my course in life. If not for them, I might not be alive to write this book.

Chapter III: Off to College, and the Next Big Thing

By my final year of high school, in 1963, I was eighteen, and up to 6'7" with a size-eighteen shoe. I was really concerned about my feet—where were they going to stop? It made me think of the Wadlow Giant. He was a man from St. Louis in the 1950's, who grew to nearly nine feet tall and weighed upwards of 450 pounds—with a *36* shoe! (You can see one of these mammoth pieces of footwear at the "Ripley's Believe It or Not!" attraction in Myrtle Beach, SC.)

Aside from my growth concerns, things were looking up. I was having a great year basketball-wise, and then, that spring, I got a big surprise, when the guidance counselor summoned me to his office. Expecting the worst, I thought: *Now what?* Though, when I was called in along with a fellow player named John Lookabaugh, we were told that several schools were inquiring about us—because they had scholarships to offer! Great news! I had twenty-eight offers, and so did John! We looked at each other in shock. But there was bad news, too: I just wasn't prepared to go to college. I'd had no idea that this could happen, being offered a scholarship on the strength of my ball-playing. The counselor even said that one of the schools was UNC—wow!

However, the matriculation process wasn't so straightforward. The only way I could go to a big school, the guidance counselor explained, was to first attend a junior college, keep a C average, and then later transfer. He had found a junior college that, if John and I were interested, would give us a chance, full ride. We could go see the school and meet the coach; the guidance counselor would make all the arrangements. It was a game-changer for me, and I couldn't believe it was happening. John and I said yes, and after the summer (during which I finished working my job at Howell's Hardware), off we went to Wesley College, all the way across the Delaware Memorial bridge in Dover, Delaware.

Once we'd arrived at the small school, John Lookabaugh and I met with a Coach Wentworth. Everything went well, and the next thing I knew, I was a college student at Wesley—a dream come true! Thus began a new chapter in the Book of Dip.

* * *

My attendance at Wesley began in 1963, and I gave it my all.

I practiced ball. I studied. I worked hard (and, thank God, my feet stopped growing!). Overall, things were good. My going off to school wasn't without its downsides, however. My brother Raymon was only seven, and it was hard leaving him; but he did at least have Mrs. Cox and Aunt B, and besides, this was the opportunity of a lifetime for me. I was the first Garrison to go to college—who knew where this might lead? The scholarship was my only shot at finding out, and I had to take it. So, school and basketball commanded my total effort.

The academic end, I had covered. The coach provided tutors if needed, to help keep my grades up; I had good professors and I kept out of trouble. But there was one little problem: Wesley College was coed. Worse, Wesley was a *Methodist church school*, attended by many kids who'd been raised in strict church homes. When *these* girls got out on their own, they were some of the wildest women I ever met. So tough to stay focused!

There was another problem, too: my finances, for I had very little money saved. But, thankfully, God intervened again. Here, Mr. Howell returned to the picture, in the form of a letter and some money I got every month, from him and some customers who chipped in a few dollars each week so that I had some spending money. Once again, they never knew what that meant to me, and what a blessing it was!

Things were going well elsewhere, too. I had another really good year with basketball, and I was able to keep at least a C average in all my classes. Better yet, I heard that the Baltimore Bullets had sent a scout to watch me play, which thrilled me to no end. Plus, I still hoped to transfer to UNC. I was on a physical upswing, too. Though no longer growing in height, I was putting on more weight, mostly in my legs.

Then spring came, and it was back home for me. I welcomed the homecoming, because it was good to see my brother, and my dad seemed to be doing better. Jack Howell had hired a replacement when I left for school, so I got a summer job loading trucks at a bread company. I also bought a motorcycle, a Triumph 650. Now I didn't have to walk or hitchhike everywhere I went. What a relief. I loved riding that bike. It's hard to believe that it would nearly cost me my life.

Yes, the motorcycle would instigate my third near-death experience. I had a friend who worked at a grocery down the street from the bread store (on the Millville-Bridgeton pike), and he had a motorcycle, too! We rode together sometimes, and one night after work I went to meet him for a ride to Bridgeton, where the Cumberland County fair was to be held. I hate to tell you why we were going there! The fair had a gorilla, and the organizers were offering $500 to anyone who could stay in the ring with him for three minutes. Upon hearing of it, I thought, *Ha! I'm 6'7", weigh 240, and can move around. I'll outrun him if I can't beat him!* For that kind of money, I would've done anything, including getting killed by a gorilla! Crazy but true. I was ready to win that $500, I tell you; I'd all but spent it. Little did I know what was about to happen that night after I left the bread company.

We never know what's around the corner—in this case, both figuratively and literally. I was on my bike and it was just turning dark. A couple minutes down the road from work, I went to turn left into the grocery store where my motorcycle friend worked. Slowing down, I looked in my mirror and turned my head, just to make sure no one was passing me—and then, before I knew it, I was staring into two oncoming headlights. The car was heading right for me, and fast. My first thought was, *You're dead!*

The car had drifted over the center line, doing an estimated sixty miles an hour, and it hit me head on. As it so happened, the driver was a seventy-year-old man, and he'd just come over a little hill fronting the grocery, which obscured visibility of the other side—the man just never saw me! Bystanders in front of the grocery said I went straight up into the air, over telephone wires that were over forty feet high, and then came straight down, head-first onto a concrete curb with no helmet. After the crash, the last thing I remembered was a sense of going "up," and I thought: *At least I'm going to Heaven.* Thankfully, I passed out before coming down. The car's elderly driver wasn't hurt.

Both the car and motorcycle were totaled—and so was I. Right off the bat, I lost about thirty pounds of flesh, from the impact alone. Then, from my crash landing, I lost about one and a half inches of height, having compacted my skeleton. Thank God I was unconscious when I hit the ground, because I simply folded up like an accordion (rather than resisting and causing further injury). Still, the accident ripped me to pieces—bad day! I was kind of surprised when I regained consciousness, lying in the gutter along the road—hadn't I been going up to Heaven? But, no, I was still alive (though life as I knew it was over).

I lifted my head and saw my body covered with blood, my flesh devastated, my right leg barely hanging on. I could see my bone from the knee down, and the *bottom* of one of my enormous feet, looking up at me! Ironically, my first concern was of basketball. *That's history,* I thought. Next, and equally bad, I remembered what my dad had said to me three weeks earlier, on my nineteenth birthday: "Son, you can do some crazy stuff, but please don't do anything *stupid*, because my insurance for you ended on your birthday and I have no money to renew it!" After that came the ambulance, and as the medics reached down to load me up, I remember looking at one of them and telling him, point blank, "Don't do it. I want to lie here and bleed to death!" This only made the medic grin as he continued loading me onto a gurney. I made a fist and drew back to hit him, but I blacked out again. I next regained consciousness in the emergency room, lying on a table, looking up at a bright white light with a doctor hovering over me. Still in my suicidal despair, I turned in his direction and shouted, "Don't you touch me, or I'll sue you for everything you've got!" The doctor turned whiter than the ceiling, and I promptly passed out again.

I found out later that my dad had been located at the American Legion, playing poker, a little ways from the hospital. With a police escort, he arrived at the hospital and signed a release to work on me, just before I bled to death. The next time I woke up was in the operating room, now with three doctors: a Dr. Davies (the one whom I'd threatened to sue), plus a pair of new ones. The two others were preparing to amputate my right leg, but Dr. Davies, standing between them and me, told them, "No, you can't take his leg. He's a basketball player." And that was the last thing I heard until later on, as I was being wheeled into my room. I overheard one nurse tell another: "Don't leave any clothes in here, or he's likely to disappear on us again!" Apparently, they remembered my previous stay, from five years before, when I'd recovered from my infection and gone AWOL for my ballgame.

The headline of next day's Millville paper read: "Dipper Loses Leg & Maybe His Life in Motorcycle Accident!" Needless to say, I didn't lose either—thanks to Dr. Davies. That man wasn't there by accident, like so many others who intervened to save my life. I didn't know him, but I used to walk by his house, an old, rundown place with a similarly decrepit car out front, on the way to basketball practice. I knew that a doctor lived there, and often wondered why one would live in such a place (aren't doctors supposed to be rich?). While in the hospital, I got my answer: Dr. Davies was 53 years old, and had had three heart attacks because he worked around the clock, day and night, refusing to stop. He was a Christian, and was supporting third-world hospitals all over the globe! Presumably, that explained his humble property. What a man he was!

My recovery was long and slow, taking me nearly two years alone to get over the concussion from my 40-foot fall to the concrete curb (my wife says I still haven't recovered from that part). In the end, those two other doctors didn't get their way with my leg. Dr. Davies worked on it every day, unable to give up on saving it from amputation—and he was successful, thank God! But, Dr. Davies did more than save my leg.

My last day in the hospital, he came into my room and said, "Dipper, you're going home today and you won't believe what happened— the hospital says they can't find your bill!" Shocked, I answered, "They can't find my bill?!" Dr. Davies went on: "Because the hospital can't find your bill, we doctors also can't find ours, so you don't owe anything and are free to leave!" He then laughed and started out the door, leaving me speechless in my room. Of course, I realized something strange was going on, with the hospital "losing" a massive bill. It was obvious I was being done a favor (though I dared not acknowledge this; one reason I'd wanted to be left for dead was because I didn't want to burden my dad with the hospital expenses).

"Doctor Davies, how can I ever repay you?" I asked, making him stop and turn around. "Son," he said then, "you don't have a clue what I'm about to say, but someday I want you to tell people what Jesus did for you, for it's only because of Him that you're alive and don't owe us anything— and that you have a leg to walk out of here with today!" As you read this book, I guess I just repaid that debt (or some interest on it, at least).

That day, I was discharged from the hospital with a metal brace on my leg, going from my knee and running into my shoe. I had nine pins in my ankle, holding it together. I didn't walk too good, but, praise God, I *did* walk out! As for Dr. Davies, he went on to work for many years. The last I heard about him was in a phone call, 33 years later, from the hospital I'd been taken to after my accident. I thought they were calling to tell me that Dr. Davies had died, but, instead, it was his son on the line. "Dipper," the man said, "you won't believe what happened today!" When I asked what happened, he told me that Dr. Davies had *retired* (and that he, the son, was taking over for him)! At the time, Dr. Davies was still alive and well.

* * *

Before closing this chapter, I'd like to make two points about my accident.

First, I realized afterward that the Lord had wanted me to get to the fairgrounds that night—not to meet the gorilla, but a *girl*! (More on that later.) Second, I've concluded that my motorcycle accident was probably allowed by God, because of two possibilities: one, that if I'd gotten to the fair, the gorilla would've killed me; or, two, the gorilla was a Christian, and the Lord thought I might kill *him*!

Chapter IV: Life After Basketball

My career as a ballplayer was over before it really began. But, like always, life went on.

Good news arrived after I left the hospital: Coach Wentworth from Wesley called to inform me that even if my injuries kept me from basketball, the college would still honor my scholarship. So I went back to Wesley and, eventually, graduated the junior college. Soon after, another good thing happened: I fell in love and got engaged. A fellow graduate, her name was Pam, and her family lived in St. Louis, where her father was a vice president at Union Carbide. After graduation, in 1965, Pam went home to St. Louis, and I followed (though I had no idea what to do there other than get married!).

St. Louis was difficult from the start. First, to get there with my duffel bag and one suitcase, it took all the money I had. Second, when I finally got to Pam's house, I could tell right away that her parents were not impressed with me. To them, I was a lowborn farm boy—a hick from the sticks. Admittedly, I wasn't looking too good, with my bad right leg, which lent me a slight limp that I would carry for life. My future wasn't looking too good, either.

To their credit, Pam's parents tried to be pleasant, considering the situation. They allowed me to stay at their home until I could find a place, and a couple days later I was invited to the country club with the family, for dinner. This, too, didn't go well. I had no manners, no appropriate clothes; I'd never been to a country club or any sort of fancy place. To say that I didn't fit in would be an understatement. Worse, I made a major mistake: after the waiter brought me the expensive squab dinner I'd ordered, I asked for some *ketchup*—what a faux pas! I knew I was in trouble as soon as I said it, just from the way Pam's parents looked at each other, and the waiter's response. I looked to Pam for help, but received none. It was right then and there, I believe, that her parents decided I needed to be gone!

At first, however, their decision wasn't so apparent. In the meantime, I found a job at another hardware store, plus a second job, at a doughnut shop right next door. The doughnut place had a furnished apartment over top, and they rented it to me. I couldn't wait to tell Pam and her family—but it didn't matter, because Pam soon informed me that the marriage was off! As it would turn out, her father had promised her a new car, several thousand dollars, and a new wardrobe if she would get rid of me. When she gave me the news, my heart was broken again, just like when my mother had died (and, when I'd once broken up with a high-school sweetheart). I was devastated, completely wiped out. I remember going back to my new apartment and thinking, *Now what do I do?* Pam had kept me going after the accident, and now it was over between us—plus I was still in St. Louis, with no one and no money.

I reacted badly. I got my rifle out of my duffel bag, chambered a shell, and sat at the kitchen table in my apartment. I stuck the gun barrel in my mouth and put my thumb on the trigger. I don't think I wanted to die, necessarily; like most suicides, I just wanted the pain to stop, and didn't know any other way to stop it. I was basically crazy at that moment, not thinking clearly at all, at the end of my rope. But, thankfully, God was looking over me, so that I had only another *near*-death experience, rather than the real deal.

No, I didn't chicken out at the last moment: I did, in fact, pull the trigger with the gun in my mouth. I remember pushing down with my thumb, then everything going dark. A couple hours later, I awoke, alive, with the gun lying on the floor beside me—it had never gone off! In a bewildered daze, I found myself reviewing my life, and it brought some important things to light. Mainly, I realized that Pam and her family had done the right thing; I wasn't really ready for marriage, nor was I the right person for her. Next, I thought about all the people who cared about me and had helped out over the years. Last, I realized that St. Louis could still work: I had two jobs and a place to live, and people who loved me (albeit in Jersey). Also, I had *time*, 24 hours a day with no responsibilities. The best thing I could do, I decided, was to take advantage of the situation, which would provide some money plus take my mind off the heartbreak.

So, I had my plan. I started the next morning, at the hardware store, where I worked from 8:00 AM to 4:00 PM, throwing myself into the job. I then walked across the street to the doughnut shop and did the same thing there (which was doubly good, because the doughnuts were the best in the world, and the owner had given me permission to eat all I wanted!). I worked nonstop, and liked it so much that my two jobs weren't enough. While on break from the doughnut place one night, I noticed a "HELP WANTED" sign at a nearby gas station, and so I got that job, too, pumping gas from midnight to 8:00 AM. (By the way: at this time, gas was $0.19 a gallon. Folks would bring their VW's in, fill up for a couple dollars, and be good for a week—try that now!) But even there I didn't stop. On my day off, I walked a few blocks to a golf course that needed caddies, and hired on

18

there part-time—a grand total of three fulltime jobs, plus the caddying (which, as a bonus, helped build my leg back up).

When I tell this story, people often ask how I could've managed this juggling act. Well, first off, the jobs were all right there together, saving me transit time. Also, I didn't work them all on the same days. The key, however, was the gas station job: because I worked the graveyard shift, most of the night was slow, so I could sit down and sleep until the bell went off and alerted me to a customer. The only problem was those doughnuts I was making, and the fact that I ate them for free. After nine months had passed (the time I'd intended to stay in St. Louis before heading home), I'd built up a belly from eating so many. I'd never been so out of shape. I remember telling God that if He could only get me back in school somewhere, I'd get myself back together. It was a hard request to make, for I was still mad at God for taking my dear, praying mother.

Before I go further, you must first hear about how I got a car.

In case you're wondering why the doughnut shop owner didn't mind me eating all those doughnuts, there's a good explanation: I was the only person he'd ever hired who hadn't stopped eating the doughnuts after a couple weeks. Also, he didn't really care how many were sold, nor did he even advertise the store, because it was all just a mob front. The truth came out when I mentioned that I was saving money to buy a car, after which the owner introduced me to two friends of his. Turned-out fellows, in suits and hats like the Blues Brothers, each with a neat little briefcase, these men happened to have a car for sale: a green, one-year-old Lincoln Continental, low miles and loaded, all for $1,000. During one of their regular visits to the shop, the owner told them I was interested, and that I couldn't smell (a lasting effect of the fever I'd had during that life-threatening super-infection as a teenager). Only when they showed me the car did I understand the relevance of this fact. See, the catch was that the car's owner had been shot dead behind the wheel, then left there for two weeks. The mob men had gotten rid of the body and cleaned out the car, but they still had a problem: the smell! But, no problem for me. I bought the car.

So, after a few months in St. Louis, I had some wheels, some money saved up, and my leg was pretty much healed (along with the concussion and other damage, too). Before long, it was time to head back to Millville, NJ. I left in early spring. I was so glad to see my family again, and I set about beginning another new chapter of my life. Chiefly, I needed to find a four-year school and get back in shape. In the meantime, I got a summer job at the Wheaton Glass plant in town, where my dad worked. How far I'd come, compared to that night I almost shot myself!

Again I thought: *What comes next?*

Chapter V: A Fateful Phone Call

It was at the glass plant that I had yet another brush with death. This time, an occupational hazard.

My first day working at Wheaton Glass, I was with a group of new summer employees when the guy in charge took us around to the glass-heating tanks. These were where the sand used to make glass is heated to extremely high temperatures, and each was the size of a small room in a house—and, after every use, these hellish little chambers had to be *cleaned out*! Bingo, a job for Dip. The boss man showed us how to do it, then gave us the proper tools. When I entered my first tank, the heat hit me like a fist. After fifteen minutes, I was soaked with sweat, and after a couple hours, I was thinking it to be the worst job ever! The work was grueling, and I was soon on the brink of collapse—but still I went on, because no heating tank was going to get the best of me.

Hours passed, and when the foreman at last stuck his head in my tank to look around, he shouted, "Get out of there!" Shaking his head, he scolded: "Didn't I tell you to only work fifteen minutes, then take a fifteen-minute break? It's well over a hundred degrees in that tank! You could've *died* being in there all that time!" I said that he in fact *hadn't* told me, which was the truth; I would've worked the whole eight hours in there if he hadn't checked back.

At that point, the foreman gave me a good, long look, and I thought I was fired. Instead, he surprised me by saying, "You just got promoted." I was made head of the summer workers, and from there, I was off to the races!

So, I was back home and had a good job, and life was rolling along. Really, the only thing I lacked was a new school for the fall—but that would soon change, by way of a strange, seemingly insignificant phone call. (Do we ever really notice when the Hand of God is setting things in motion?)

The call was like the other life-changing "coincidences" I'd experienced. (I now spell coincidence "G-O-D.") It was from Wesley College's football coach, who I was acquainted with but didn't really know.

He was fairly young, and was doing some graduate studies in North Carolina, someplace called Boone. The school he attended was Appalachian Teacher's College (now Appalachian State University), with some 3,300 students, and this coach's call was the first I'd heard of it. The situation was strange from the beginning, with this mere acquaintance inviting me down to some backwater town in another state. As we were talking, I couldn't understand why the man was calling me to begin with, much less going on and on about this school he wanted me to visit. I don't even know how he knew my phone number! Needless to say, I wasn't at all interested, and I told him so. We said our goodbyes, and I hung up.

But it didn't stop there.

A few days later, the Wesley coach called back—and again pestered me about seeing this North Carolina town named Boone! And, again, I said, "Not interested. Goodbye." Yet the man *still* wasn't done, for he soon called a third time. "Dipper," he said then, "I'm not going to call again. Actually, I don't know why I'm calling you at all, but I'll just tell you this: there's thirty-three hundred students, and around two thirds of them are *girls*!" Girls: the magic word. "Why didn't you say that in the first place?!" I replied. "I'll be right down!"

And that's how I arrived in Boone, NC, in the middle of July, 1966.

No, I'd never heard of Boone. I barely knew of the Appalachian mountains in which the rural town was nestled. I'd never been farther south than a trip to some caverns in Virginia. But there I was, in this sleepy little mountain town, on the tip of a man I hardly knew. At a glance, Boone looked like a little paradise. The temperatures were in the seventies when I got there, and everything was a dark, lush green—I loved it! The school seemed nice, and Wesley's football coach had been right: lots of girls! He and I met up briefly on my first day there, but I never saw him again. Boone, on the other hand, would be in my life for decades thereafter.

Smitten, I submitted an application to Appalachian Teacher's College, then returned to New Jersey. Two weeks later, I was accepted to the school. I was thrilled with the news, and couldn't wait to get back to Boone and its thriving population of coeds. Impressed, I called some guys from Wesley and, like the football coach, told them what I'd found in North Carolina. All four of my friends applied and were accepted, and we agreed to meet up in late August and then look for a place to stay. Suddenly everything was working out. The good times had returned, and life felt great again!

Before I started attending Appalachian Teacher's College, however, one more big thing was to happen up in Jersey: I would meet the woman I was to marry!

* * *

22

My marriage, also, started out small.

One Friday in August, 1966, while I was finishing up my job at Wheaton Glass during my last few weeks up north, a coworker invited me out to a bar. I told him no, because I didn't like this guy too much, but he begged me, not giving up. He wanted to meet up with a girl from his college but didn't want to show up alone. Still, I declined a second time, now because I'd previously been thrown out of the bar in question and told never to return (for fighting). But then, after work that night, the guy approached me again, now *pleading* with me to go with him. That time, I changed my mind, I don't know why (felt sorry for him, I guess). I told my coworker that if they'd let me in the door, I'd go to the bar. Little did I know what lay in store for me there.

Upon arriving with me at the bar that night, my coworker spotted his woman at a table with some girlfriends, and we sat down. He introduced me to the group, and we exchanged hellos and small talk. I was sitting next to the prettiest girl at the table, a smiling brunette named Charlotte, in a modest-but-attractive dress. In just a few minutes, I'd asked her out on a date for the following evening. She gave me her phone number but failed to get mine—which was a good thing, for by the next day she'd had a change of heart about the date, and would've feigned sickness had she been able to reach me. But, due to her mistake, she was stuck with me! (Another "God thing.")

And here's some additional irony: when I went to pick Charlotte up, guess where she lived? Right across from *the fairgrounds*, my destination on the fateful night of my motorcycle accident. Yes, I was supposed to get to those fairgrounds after all—not to wrestle a gorilla, but to meet Charlotte, my bride to be. Also, there was another coincidence in our meeting: parallels between Charlotte's mother and my own. Both were named Pearl, were sweet Christian women with good-but-unbelieving husbands, and were similar in other respects. *Sound familiar?* I thought. I was really knocked off my feet when I met Charlotte's mother for the first time, and I couldn't help but warm to her. In some ways, it was like having my own mom back.

Chapter VI: It's Always Something

Once I'd finally met the ravishing young Charlotte, my life again changed course.

Our courtship went well. We dated for the rest of my time in Jersey, and were soon a proper couple, such that we remained attached when I left for Boone to resume my schooling. Our relationship complicated my departure, for not only was I again saying goodbye to my family, but now Charlotte too. But, however difficult, the goodbyes were said, and off I went.

I arrived in Boone looking forward to what life there might bring. I really couldn't believe the place, such was its allure. My personal situation was good, also. Even after paying my tuition, I still had money to set aside for the coming year. I got back with the four Wesley buddies whom I'd referred to Boone, and we found a cabin fairly close to campus. Soon we were moved in, enrolled in school, and everything was rolling along. I was majoring in physical education (with a minor in psychology), and I started working out at the campus gym—an ideal arrangement. On top of everything, Charlotte was coming down to see me. This last part, however, would prove disastrous.

Charlotte's actual visit was fine. She stayed in Boone a week, and we had a great time. The problem involved her car. A beautiful 1964 Chevy Malibu convertible, it begged to be driven, so I talked Charlotte into letting me borrow it. Our arrangement was, she would fly home, then I'd bring the Malibu back up when I came to visit on Thanksgiving—no problem, right? She pleaded with me to take good care of it, and I promised I would. The last thing she said before leaving was, "Don't let anything happen to my car, or my dad will kill me!" I repeated my promise, and away she went.

A few days later, it was a beautiful, warm summer day, and I decided to go driving with a friend named Bill. We got in the Malibu and put the top down—still no problem, right? We drove out to a place called Hilltop, about a mile out of town, and it was there that things went south. I saw an oncoming car as we approached, and from the way this car was moving, I could tell it wasn't going to slow or stop for anything. Then *another* car appeared—in the other lane, passing the first. It was coming right at us as if playing chicken, and there was nowhere to go; I remember telling Bill to hold on to something. I had a choice: a head-on collision with the passing car, or go over the cliff at roadside. In the heat of the moment, I chose the cliff, and over the trees we flew. Miraculously, we landed without flipping, and neither I nor Bill were hurt. The car, on the other hand, wasn't so fortunate.

The very next day, I began Operation Cover-up, to repair the car and avoid upsetting Charlotte's father. While living in Boone, I had met a man named Cook, and he had a body shop just nearby. I went to him and explained the situation: that I'd promised this girl I wouldn't let anything happen to her car; that I had to drive it back to Jersey come Thanksgiving; the impending wrath of Charlotte's father. Mr. Cook asked me how much money I had, which was about $1,100 at the time. He agreed to fix the car for that amount, and I handed it over. Mr. Cook did a great job, having the Malibu ready to go before Thanksgiving. Afterward, my only problem was that I now had no money for the rent! I did, at least, successfully return the car, after which I visited with my family and then hitchhiked back to Boone.

Back in town, I returned to my previous problem: no rent money. When I told my roommates from Wesley, they were without sympathy, and I was informed that I couldn't stay in the cabin. I remember walking to town after being kicked out, and all I had to my name was a five-dollar bill. Wandering around, I came upon the college campus and, eventually, the school's football stadium. There, I found a hole in the ground along the stadium's west wall, and this became my new home. Later, I visited an Army surplus store downtown, where my five dollars bought a blanket and a sleeping bag. The good times were at an end. *This isn't going to be fun*, I thought!

Unfortunately, back in those days, there wasn't much help available for someone in my position. One church heard about me, and they let me come inside after the Wednesday-night service and its subsequent dinner, from which I received the leftovers. I could usually get two or three days' worth of meals from there; other than that, I ate whatever I could find, which wasn't much. Charlotte once sent a cake to my old house, and the guys were good enough to see that I got it! I ate the whole thing within a day.

Come winter, my situation had not improved. As balmy and pleasant as Boone had been that summer, it was as cold and miserable in the off season. Plus, that the winter I spent homeless was *especially* cold, the worst in years (according to the locals). There was always snow on the ground, from when I moved into my hole at the stadium until I left for Christmas break. Many nights I thought I was going to freeze to death; mornings, I'd often awake to find myself so frozen I couldn't walk. I would literally crawl over to the gym, then thaw out in the shower—oh, I loved that shower. I kept going to classes, since my tuition was paid up, and a lot of my time was spent in the school library. But once that closed, it was back to my cold, lonely hole!

Amazingly, I did manage to finish the semester and pass the exams; but I'd started breaking down. Combined with the homelessness, the physical and mental distress truly drained my energies. The longer I spent outside in the cold, malnourished and stressed, the more it wore me down, until I became delirious, unable to keep going. It was only a matter of time, then. Before I could succumb, however, God intervened!

Somehow—to this day I'm not quite sure how—I ended up on a bus, with a note pinned to my chest. The bus was northbound, heading out of Boone, and the note on my chest had written on it a phone number, with instructions that it be called once I reached Bridgeton, NJ. When I arrived, some Samaritan called the number, said "There's a gift for you at the bus station," and hung up. The recipient of the call then drove down to the bus station, expecting a box or present of some type; instead, there was only me, totally out of it, nothing but skin and bone (I'd dropped from around 230 pounds to 185). The phone number on the note was, of course, Charlotte's.

By this time, Charlotte had written me off. After I wrecked her car, her father was furious with both of us (he'd seen through the ruse, despite Mr. Cook's great repair job), and Charlotte had told me she never wanted to see me again. We stopped corresponding sometime after I'd returned her car at Thanksgiving, and, except for that cake she'd sent, I'd heard nothing from her. So, when she saw me instead of the nonexistent gift, it was something of a miracle that she didn't turn right around and leave.

Instead, Charlotte took one look at me, and her heart broke. At once, she drove me home and nursed me back to health—and would later marry me (and we'd stay together for 45 years)! What a way to get a wife: first our unlikely meeting at the bar, then her picking me up at a bus station with a note pinned to my chest (when I'd wrecked her car to boot)! I don't recommend getting your spouse this way.

* * *

With plenty of home cooking and TLC, I did indeed recover from my troublesome winter, as did my relationship with Charlotte. Life went on.

After getting back on my feet, I wasted no time finding a job, now as a car salesman at a Chevy dealership called Scribner and Lewis. My partner there was a man with a unique name: John Toothaker, pronounced "tooth-ay-ker." He would introduce himself with, "It's my name, not my condition," and the line worked well for him (a car salesman thrives on being remembered by name). The trade was new to me, but I had no problem learning, especially under John's guidance. He taught me much about business and life both—one of a kind, that man! We sold a lot of cars, and I moved up quickly at the car dealership. I just about lived on the lot, in time selling enough cars that I was given a brand-new one to drive. Unfortunately, all this working meant I wasn't exercising, and I ate a lot of coffee and doughnuts. It was St. Louis all over again.

In the fall of 1967 I at last returned to school, still at Appalachian Teacher's College in Boone. That year was another uptick for me, in several ways. Financially, I did well enough as a car salesman that I had that brand-new set of wheels I'd mentioned, a white 62' Corvette. Plus, I was totally healed up from my motorcycle accident and my homeless period. I was doing pretty good, all told. By the time I returned to Boone for school, the town was growing, in a boom, as if the whole world was discovering it like I had. The school had built a new, modern gym, with a great weight room, and it became my second home; I was able to fulfill my promise to God to get back in shape. And get in shape I did: my arms were soon as big or bigger than my legs, and my waist was back to 32". I felt so much better. That year, I worked part-time at a local ski resort, and the job was easy in my upgraded condition, no sweat. I finished up a couple more quarters at school, then went back to Bridgeton to see my family and my new love, Charlotte.

It was then, on this particular return home, that I got one of my more interesting jobs: with a repo company.

Being a repo man was pretty straightforward. They gave me a big truck, a couple of helpers, and a list of names and addresses, and then sent me on my way. I got an hourly wage, plus a bonus on everything I successfully repossessed. Most of the targeted stuff was furniture, kitchen appliances, and other housewares, along with some lawnmowers and jewelry and the like. I was pretty good at the job, as it turned out; my size helped a lot. However, I didn't stay in the business for long, because of some tough lessons I learned on the job. Namely, that it's hard to be a repo man and still be human, to still "have a heart."

The turning point came when I went out to repo a kitchen—the *whole* kitchen. All appliances were on my list. The insolvent owner, a woman in her early forties with five kids and no husband, was home when I arrived. When I told her I'd come for her kitchen stuff, she begged me not to take it. The refrigerator had food in it, and she was cooking on the stove. I felt sorry for her, and she soon grabbed onto me and cried, "What am I going to do?! How will I feed my kids?! This is all I have left!" Without answering, my guys and I took everything out of the fridge, gently removed the meal from the stove, then loaded everything into the truck while the woman sat with her kids and cried.

It would be my last repo. By the time I got back to the shop, my heart was aching for that poor woman and her family. I felt for her so much, I asked the boss how much she owed on that stuff, and, when he gave me a figure, I said to deduct it from my check. I then proceeded to turn the truck around and return to the woman's house. She was still home, and when I told her that I'd paid her bill, then began bringing her stuff back in, I can't describe her joy. My helpers and I were bombarded with thank-you's. Once back at the repo shop, I went to my boss, handed over the keys to the truck, and said "I quit." My heart had softened.

* * *

Soon after my stint as a repo man, I decided to return to school. I told Charlotte and my family, and we again exchanged somber goodbyes, though it wasn't so hard as before. My brother Raymon seemed to be doing well; Dad was in love with Eleanor, his bride to be; my Aunt Beulah was happy for me, which meant a lot. Charlotte was another story, of course, but I was able to pry myself away. When I left for Boone this time, it was in style: I had a gold 68' Corvette Stingray, and I looked good in it. I just plain looked good, too. I'd done well repo-ing, and I had kept working out. All was right in the world, it seemed—but you ought to know by now that something was about to change that, right?

Believe it or not, I had another car accident.

It was a beautiful sunny day, perfect for the drive back south. I was on Highway 81, about halfway to Boone, when I came upon a big bend in the dual-lane highway, with a forest of large trees on my right. That's when things went wrong. From what I can piece together, my error was simple: I fell asleep. The next thing I knew, a cop was looking down on me, and all that was left of that frail, fiberglass Corvette was the frame and the steering column—and me, experiencing a rude awakening in the driver's seat. The rest of the car was gone; behind me lay a path of mowed-down trees. Yet I again escaped with my life; in fact, I wasn't hurt at all. I remember the cop saying, "I don't know what happened, but I can't believe you're alive!" The man was so stunned, he didn't even write me a ticket. Though I was heartbroken about losing the Corvette (I loved that car), the accident barely fazed me. Afterward, I just found my bag, then hitchhiked back to Boone, thankful to still be alive. Fall off the horse, get back on.

Soon I was back in school at Appalachian Teacher's College. For work, I was now in charge of that fancy new weight room they'd built on campus, and I returned to the ski slopes on a part-time basis. That year, I really got into the weights—heavy lifting now, outright bodybuilding. I got bigger; I bought another car; I did good in school—a good winter. By spring, I was ready to swing back to Bridgeton, and it was on this trip that I asked Charlotte to marry me! She said yes, and suddenly I had a sweet, pretty fiancé, who was so good to me that I had to make sure I wasn't dreaming. With that, things couldn't have been better. We decided to marry in August, then return to Boone so I could finish my degree.

Of course, the engagement complicated my life somewhat. No more running around, no more partying, no more of those delightful Boone coeds. I was engaged to a good, sweet choirgirl, and it was time to leave the old life behind—"settle down and grow up" time. It was a new experience, but ultimately I felt good about it. I felt good about my family, too; my brother was now a teenager, and Dad was still on his way to his second wife. Life moved fast for me at this point, with its ups and downs and twists and turns. But I held on through the ride—what a trip! Just like that, it was August of 1969, and I was getting married.

Charlotte was a beautiful bride, even though she didn't wear a wedding gown. You see, by then I'd kind of turned into a hippy ("Hippy Dippy" I was called), and all I had to wear were some jeans and a white shirt, without so much as a tie. So, to match my casual attire, Charlotte opted for a simple bridesmaid dress. Ironically, I ended up wearing a tux after all, thanks to a cousin who fixed me up (complete with dress shoes, even)—but this would backfire! When I showed up to the wedding service in this getup, it was even worse than wearing jeans. You should've seen the look on Charlotte's face! She'd sacrificed an elaborate wedding dress for me, and I'd gone and gotten dressed up without telling her. Thankfully, it wasn't a deal-breaker for the marriage, and the service was otherwise a success (though I'm still in trouble for this "indiscretion," 45 years later!).

Chapter VII: The Married Life

After the marriage, I moved back to Boone, now with my new wife in tow. I still had a year of school left.

I know the move was hard on Charlotte, with her having to leave Bridgeton after living there her whole life. The most difficult thing for her, I think, was having to separate from her mother, Pearl, because they were so close. Worse, Pearl was concerned that her only child, a lifelong Baptist choirgirl, was marrying an unbelieving, down-and-out hick who barely had a nickel to his name! All the same, Charlotte's mother was very kind and gracious to me, even with all my faults—I'd go so far as to say the woman loved me. The same could not be said of Charlotte's father. His name was Burt, and I don't think he ever did like me, even before I wrecked Charlotte's Malibu. Unlike Pearl, he only tolerated me, and only then because he didn't have a choice, I think. So the move south was a bit of an issue, our marriage's first; but we worked through it.

Another little road bump came in regards to my age. At the time of our marriage, Charlotte was 26 and I was 24, but I'd previously led her to believe I was older, in a little white lie while we were dating (out of fear that she wouldn't date a younger man). When the truth came out, she was disconcerted, I think by the simple fact that I misled her. But she did eventually accept that she'd robbed the cradle, just as she had the move to Boone. To this day, she jokingly rolls her eyes whenever I bring up my "fib."

It didn't take us long to get established in Boone. By the winter following our wedding in August of '69, we'd moved into our own little castle: a cozy 8'-by-32' trailer, bought on our wedding money (about $1,000). It was in a trailer park, in what was then the outskirts of Boone, just behind an upscale steakhouse called The Peddler. We traded in our respective cars for a blue 69' Dodge Charger, and we didn't wreck it. Things were good, and Charlotte and I were cruising along, making it in the world. In fact, things were, for me, the best they'd ever been, what with having a house and a car and the girl of my dreams. I thought I'd died and gone to Heaven!

How could life get any better? Well, Charlotte did need a job.

She set about finding work soon after we'd moved into our little love nest, and the job she found was another godsend. Having always been a secretary, Charlotte now wanted to do something else. I asked around, and a friend told me that The Peddler Steakhouse had just opened and they needed another waitress—the same Peddler we were living right behind! It would be the perfect arrangement. Charlotte applied the next day, and was hired on the spot. The restaurant's owner was a man named Bob Roschy, who had recently moved to Boone with his wife, and he'd just finished building the steakhouse before Charlotte and I had left New Jersey. After hiring Charlotte, Bob started her right away.

The Peddler was a new franchise, and still small, but you haven't been to a steakhouse until you've experienced a Peddler. They would come to your table with a fresh-cut loin, cut it to your liking, then cook it on live charcoal while you went to a salad bar—all at the cost of $4.95. What a deal! Charlotte loved the job, and the folks at The Peddler loved her. The restaurant was open every night from 6:00 to 10:00, and she never missed a day's work, always determined to make a happy customer. And afterward, she could just walk the short distance to our trailer. The job couldn't have been better suited to her. The Hand of God had once again been at work.

Chapter VIII: Who Would Have Guessed?!

After the excitement of love and marriage and buying our trailer, I was back in school, hoping to graduate in the spring.

I was still lifting weights, and I'd gotten pretty strong by then, enough to compete. In one competition, I broke the NC dead-lift record, which was over 650 pounds! I was also doing impressive weights on the arm curls: 285 pounds, with 22-inch arms. Coincidentally, that was the same weight Arnold Schwarzenegger was lifting at the time. Once, I went to a pawnshop to look at a gun, and they had a dumbbell that weighed over 100 pounds. The owner, seeing me eyeballing the dumbbell, made an offer: "If you can curl that five times, I'll give you that gun you were looking at." I promptly curled the dumbbell five times, then walked out of the pawn shop with a free gun. About that same time, my size brought about a small brush with fame: I was asked to spar with Mohammad Ali, who was, then, the heavyweight champion of the world. We met, and I remember him looking at my arms, then looking up at me. The next thing I knew, the sparring match was cancelled—chicken!

My life's next big twist involved The Peddler, that restaurant we'd coincidentally moved behind just before Charlotte started working there.

It was around 8:00 on a Saturday night, and I was at home in the trailer, watching TV, when Charlotte arrived home unexpectedly from work. "Dipper," she said at once, "we're slammed and the dishwasher didn't show up. Bob wants to know if you'll come wash dishes. He'll pay, and feed you too!" I liked Bob (he was a good boss), so I said that I'd be right there. Charlotte ran back to The Peddler, and I got dressed and soon followed her, entering the restaurant's back door. As soon as Bob learned I was there, he appeared back in the kitchen, thanked me for coming, and showed me how to operate the dishwasher. With that, Bob returned to the grill, and I was left with my work.

The restaurant certainly was slammed, going by how many dishes I washed; but I was up to the task. So, when Bob at last returned to check up on me, a couple hours later, he appeared shocked: I was on top of my work, with everything neat and put away. Knowing I'd never washed dishes before, Bob had expected disarray; instead, I was standing by an empty washing machine, scrubbing it down and looking quite collected—which I was. No sweat off my brow, this dishwashing thing! Bob couldn't believe it, and at the end of the night, he reappeared in the kitchen, now with a big smile on his face. "Great job, Dipper," he said to me. "You ready to eat?" Music to my ears! I was shown to the dining room, and told I could have anything I wanted, free. I had my first Peddler steak and salad bar that night, after which I was paid cash. Later, Charlotte told me that Bob couldn't get over how I'd handled the dishes, and how impressed he was with me.

Little did I know, that night would prove to be my ticket into the restaurant business.

I learned more about Bob Roschy as Charlotte and I spent more time with him. He'd come to Boone from Las Vegas, a gambler who'd supported himself as a waiter. Back west, he'd suffered gambling losses to the point of finding himself on a park bench one day, broke, hung over, and ready to call it quits. He'd then headed east and married his wife, Shirley, who had a little money. He somehow learned of the Peddler franchise, and that's how the Boone Peddler came to be. For him, golf was another draw to Boone, with the town having several resorts. If Bob liked anything, it was gambling and golf. At the time I met him, he was about 30 years old.

Soon after that night I washed dishes at The Peddler, I had an "Aha!" moment. Charlotte came home one evening, and she'd just been paid, including all the night's tips. She counted everything, gave me a figure (a good one)—and then handed me all her money! When I asked her how much she wanted back, she thought a minute, looked me in the eye, and said, "Well, I used to get a magazine called *Southern Living*. I think it's around four dollars for the subscription." My dear, sweet wife was working her butt off, and all she wanted out of it was a four-dollar magazine subscription! *I've got a real keeper here*, I thought, probably with the same look of disbelief that Bob had upon finding all the dishes cleaned that night. I felt very loved, and it took me a few moments to get a grip on who I'd married.

Afterward, I remember sitting Charlotte down and asking her what she was looking for in our marriage and in life (which I should've done before marrying her, I guess). She didn't mind working until she had children, she replied, after which she would like to be an at-home mom. Also, she expressed a desire to build a house, then proceeded to show me some plans she'd already bought. My thoughts were, *I've married the most unbelievable woman in the world.* If this was what she wanted, I was going to give it to her! That night, Charlotte and I agreed on our goals, and I committed to make them happen, whatever the cost!

I was off to the races again, and married life was great. Up in Jersey, my dad had remarried, to his beloved Eleanor, a good woman who loved him with all her heart; my teenage brother now had a mother again. I'd graduated from college—first Garrison ever—and I was even in grad school. Can you believe it? But, as good as things were, they hadn't really gotten moving yet, for I still had yet to experience the next twist in my story: the restaurant business.

* * *

After my night dishwashing at The Peddler, Bob Roschy asked me if I'd like to work there part-time. I said, "So long as you feed me," to which he agreed. So, I now had that going for me, making things in Boone were even better!

One night after work, Bob asked Charlotte and me to sit down with him.

By this time, there were probably a dozen Peddlers, with the Boone location the busiest of them all. Likewise, my wife was known as the top Peddler waitress—born to wait tables, was Charlotte! Her personality was simply perfect for the job, and she would often wash dishes and do other work around the restaurant, too! This was the context to Bob sitting us down to talk, after-hours at The Peddler, when everyone else had cleared out. He began: "You guys know how much you've grown on me—you're the best I could ask for! So I want you to know that I and some partners are going to put a Peddler in Williamsburg, VA, and we'd like to offer you two the final partnership." Then came the clincher: "And we want you and Charlotte to run the new restaurant!" Charlotte and I looked at each other, and all I could think was, *Wow, is this for real?* Who could've ever guessed at this turn in the road—and all stemming from a night of dishwashing?!

But, there was one issue: money. Before Charlotte and I could answer, Bob added that we would have to come up with $5,000. That was big money in those days, the equivalent of a couple new cars. At that, I told him that Charlotte and I would have to think about it. In parting, Bob informed us that we'd have to make a decision soon, because construction on the Williamsburg Peddler had already begun! I told him I understood, and Charlotte and I left.

Afterward, we stayed awestruck, unable to believe the opportunity. We could barely sleep that night! The next day, we talked it over, and agreed on the potential we were facing. We were keen to running a Peddler, to be sure, but there was a big downside: we'd have to leave Boone. Plus, there was the money. We had $2,500 saved up, but that was only half the buy-in—where would we get $2,500 on short notice? The solution came from an unlikely source: Charlotte's father, Burt. The decision to proposition the man—not my biggest fan, even after the marriage—was not taken lightly; but, surprisingly, he agreed to lend us the money. Maybe it was because I asked him long-distance, over the phone (or maybe I was growing on him the same way I had Bob!).

Immediately after securing the loan and hanging up the phone, I went to Bob to tell him that Charlotte and I were in—ready with the money, ready to ship off to Williamsburg and run a Peddler there. What a great curveball life had thrown us!

Chapter IX: A Wonderful Life in Virginia

Now begins the Williamsburg, VA, chapter of my life.

Things moved fast once we decided to pursue the Peddler partnership, in 1971. Soon after confirming the deal with Bob Roschy, Charlotte and I sold our little trailer, packed up our stuff, and headed north to Williamsburg, a place I'd never been before. My only regret was in leaving Boone, especially since I was still one quarter short of finishing my graduate degree. But Bob was insistent that we get up to Virginia ASAP, because they were finishing the building and wanted to open soon.

Unfortunately, the Williamsburg Peddler would not open as soon as expected.

We arrived at Williamsburg two days after departing Boone, and instead of finding a restaurant that was almost completed, we were met by only a concrete slab in the middle of an open property—no one around, nothing! At once, I called Bob to tell him what we'd found, and he sounded shocked. He gave me the name and number of the contractor in charge of building the restaurant, who was located in the nearby city of Newport News, and I got up with the man. The contractor had several excuses for the delay: permit problems, bad weather, other projects he'd been working on. But, he said, he was ready to begin building the new Peddler the following week—which, thankfully, he did! Phew!

Meanwhile, Charlotte and I looked for an apartment, something close to our Peddler. Somewhat miraculously, we found a place just a few days later, only a couple miles from the restaurant! We wasted no time getting squared away in our apartment, and from there began finding our way around Williamsburg. It was a lovely little town, with a college called William & Mary, and a large tourist population. Our relocation went well, and we received an additional blessing when I got some news from Bob: the other partners had agreed to pay me a small salary while we waited for the restaurant to be completed. The money really helped. Life grew comfortable.

The next couple months were lively for me. I monitored the Peddler's construction, pushing the contractor to finish up as soon as possible. I joined a gym, where I met lots of people to whom I could promote the new Peddler's grand opening. I went to every hotel, motel, and gas station in Williamsburg, distributing free dinner-for-two cards to all the staff. I targeted the low-rung workers specifically, those who pumped the gas and checked people into rooms, instead of the owners. I figured that if the working men enjoyed their meal, they'd promote the restaurant to their customers and bosses, becoming my salespeople by word of mouth. Also, I joined the Kiwanis of Williamsburg, which was a hub for all the local businessmen (one of whom was a man named Wally Riley, another key player in my story; more on him later). For someone who hadn't yet started their job, I stayed pretty busy.

The restaurant took about six months to get ready, but the big day finally arrived, and the business proved a great success. Between the locals, the college students, and the tourists, we had plenty of customers. I think that those extra months of preparation and promotion really helped, such that the delayed construction was actually a blessing in disguise. But the two biggest factors were, first, my new friend Wally Riley, who was known and loved all over the area; and, second, my wife, who wouldn't let any customer leave as anything less than satisfied. The Peddlers' best waitress had become the best hostess!

Not that we had many unsatisfied customers—hardly! We aimed to please, and we succeeded. I remember one customer in particular, a Japanese gentleman. He was so impressed, he later brought his whole family over from Japan, to enjoy the marvelous restaurant he'd discovered abroad. Of course, our success wasn't just due to the food; it was much more complicated than that, involving psychological and social elements, and even subtler things for which there are no names. All those workers I'd given the passes to, from the gas stations and hotels, were telling everyone about The Peddler—"You can't leave Williamsburg until you've experienced a Peddler steak!" It was hard to put your finger on just what made the place so good, but people liked it, whatever it was. And so the business worked.

It did so well, I had people calling me to put up a Peddler in Newport News, halfway between Williamsburg and Virginia Beach. I was also being asked to put one in Richmond, about forty miles west of Williamsburg. I reported this to the partners, and they settled on erecting a Peddler in Newport News. So, a couple years after the Williamsburg opening, we did a repeat performance in Newport News, and it wasn't long before that one was booming, too! As a matter of course, the partners and I began to consider a Richmond location. The following year, I found a restaurant that had closed down, in a great spot; with that, it was off to

Richmond. Unsurprisingly, the third endeavor was as successful as those previous.

We were doing well in our private lives, too. I was driving a snazzy convertible and wearing tailor-made suits. The Kiwanis had voted me businessman of the year. I had my wife and my house and my confidence. Could this really be happening to me? One event in particular reflects my life's upward trend at the time: when I took Charlotte for an evening at the Kennedy Center in Washington, DC. I had a tux on, with Charlotte on my arm, the two of us looking like movie stars. The sports announcer Howard Cosell was interviewing celebrities as they approached the Center, and when Charlotte and I passed by, he tried to figure out who I was and if I should be interviewed—I just had that air of success, I suppose. When we got inside, we were seated adjacent to the Kennedys themselves, and, with the way things were going for me, I felt to fit right in. Quite a night!

Around this time, I bought a new car, as successful people often do. This one, however, was a little different from those past, for it was in some sense free. See, when I'd gotten married, five years earlier, I'd decided to give up all my vices: gambling, smoking, drinking, partying. I was successful in this endeavor, and after figuring out what I would've been spending on these excesses, I began saving an equal amount daily. I called it my "vice fund," and it went in a big old coffee can. Well, at the end of those five years, I took all the money (over $11,000) to the Newport News Porsche dealership, then drove away in a brand-new set of wheels. I called it my "vice car"! Who says clean living doesn't pay?

So, Dipper wasn't doing too bad. It could be said that all my dreams were coming true, and I still couldn't quite believe it all. Yet something still seemed missing—something *inside*. I felt around this emptiness, but could never put my finger on just what it was; so, naturally, I ignored it. Of course, ignoring it didn't make it go away, and I would, later on, learn just what it was I was missing; but at the time, I just pressed on, surrounded by my worldly comforts, my wife at my side. It's so easy to ignore this sort of stuff when life is easy and you have family and friends to reassure you. (God would have to shake things up a little to get my attention.)

Speaking of friends: I will now introduce Wally Riley. During my successful venture in Virginia, he'd become a great friend and encourager. And this was no accident, for he was another of those people positioned in my life by God to help me (though I didn't know it at the time)! I learned a lot from him, the kind of real-life wisdom that is just so hard to come by. I miss Wally to this day.

He was an insurance agent by trade, for New York Life, their agent in the Williamsburg area. (His son, Mark, would eventually take over for Wally in this position, and is still going strong in the firm today.) I said earlier that Wally was known and loved all over the city; well, that stature is best summed up by the story of what happened at a business dinner one night. It was a very high-profile event, with hundreds of people in attendance, many of them VIPs—including the senator from West Virginia, Robert Byrd. During the post-meal socializing, I approached the Senator and, intent on finding my friend, asked, "Have you seen Wally Riley?" Seeing my lack of impression on meeting him, the Senator didn't know what to say; it must have been like asking the Pope where the janitor is! My wife *still* laughs when hearing this story.

* * *

So, Charlotte and I had opened our third Peddler in Virginia, and both it, and we, were doing good—things once more rolling along. I began rotating my wife around the three locations to keep business up, and it worked. Yet things had not peaked. Before long, we were opening a *second* Peddler in Williamsburg, on the other side of town—and that one filled up, too!

Though, all this success was not without its drawbacks—namely, the amount of stress I was suddenly under, keeping several busy businesses afloat. It was a juggling act, and after about four years of it, the pressure was really making itself felt. Since moving to Williamsburg, I'd only taken a couple of days off, working nonstop—I needed a vacation! *Dearly!* Yes, a trip was just what the doctor ordered.

By this time, in 1974, Charlotte and I had always dreamed of going to California, especially the Redwood forests there (the size of those trees!). So, when I went home one day and asked her if she'd like a vacation there, you can guess her answer. Not that Charlotte had voiced one complaint in our years of hard work up in Virginia. I'll say it again: what a woman! We'd had time together, since our restaurants were only open evenings, but that was no substitute for a vacation. So we were off to the Redwoods for ten days—and boy, was it necessary. The first three nights there, my body was literally vibrating with stress and tension, and it was a long time relaxing. I'd been going so fast, so long, I don't think my poor body knew how to react. By the fourth day, I finally calmed, and it was for the first time in years. I remember thinking, *I like this. I don't want to go back.*

All in all, we had a wonderful trip before returning uneventfully to Virginia. Once there, however, I wasted no time jumping right back in the game, deciding to open yet another Peddler, now in Winston Salem, NC (about a hundred miles from Boone). This venture took off like the others, and everyone seemed happy, including the partners. I liked putting these restaurants together; and, even more, I liked seeing them do so well. It was satisfying to me, an accomplishment, watching my creation grow and thrive, something like raising a competent child. On the other hand, I liked the vacation we'd taken, too, with its nourishing relaxation. So, eventually, Charlotte and I decided on another trip, now to Myrtle Beach, SC.

This trip, however, would turn out a bit differently than California, for it would begin another chapter of my life.

Chapter X: Myrtle Beach, and A New Twist

Charlotte and I fell in love with Myrtle Beach, and this is what happened.

Our romance with the place was much like my arrival in Boone all those years ago. Except, in Myrtle Beach, I set my sights on opening another Peddler, plus having a vacation home there. I was all for the new restaurant; my partners, not so much. There was, however, one who shared my zeal for the project: Murray Broome, the first manager I'd hired for the Boone restaurant (and, the best ever!). So this time it was Murray and I alone who bought the franchise. It was 1977, and we found a place in North Myrtle Beach, in the Windy Hill area, right on the ocean. Once opened, this Peddler did *really* well, just like the others. As before, Murray managed it, and he did a great job. He was married to a lady named Debbie, who was another Charlotte. (Murray got real lucky, I think.)

Peddler #5 was a success, but I still didn't stop! After opening the Myrtle Beach location and getting it squared away, I made a trip to Boone to visit Bob and see what was going on up in the mountains. While there, I learned that the property just across the street from The Peddler was for sale: an old 16-room motel called The Longvue, built around 1940. It impressed me as a good investment, maybe something I could get involved in if I ever moved back to Boone. It was something to think about, but I had my hands full, and didn't want to rush into anything. By this time, it was a decade since I'd left for Williamsburg, and I had plenty to keep me busy; but I sure missed Boone.

That brings us to my story's next unexpected twist.

Shortly after my latest visit to Boone, I went ahead and bought The Longvue, and it was then that I heard some interesting news: the Trailways bus service was looking to establish a terminal in town, which, I thought, was a perfect prospect for the motel. Because the bus service would be more for the lucrative transport of freight than of passengers (this was before the rise of UPS and Fedex), it would be ideal to run out of the less-than-picturesque motel. And this proved true, for when I did eventually get the bus service going, we got regular freight traffic, plus the guest busses; the service covered a large portion of the motel's overhead, as it turned out. And, another coincidence: the big, open parking lot was perfect for the buses, and there was a large storage area for freight. It all worked and everyone was happy—especially me, because the Trailways buses put the motel in the black. God was at work, and I didn't even know it!

Besides the motel being a good investment, I had another reason to buy it: my brother Raymon, who was now in his early twenties and working at the Newport News Peddler. I loved him with all my heart, and I wanted him somehow involved with my business back in Boone, especially since I was hoping to someday move back there—so I was overjoyed when he agreed to manage The Longvue for me. Just having him in Boone was a great blessing to Charlotte and me. My heart had never stopped hurting for Raymon, mostly because he'd never gotten a chance to know our wonderful mother—a pain that remains to this day (though he'll get to know her when he gets to Heaven, thank God!). It was a miracle that he grew up to be such a great man (and, later, a great husband and father), considering all that he had against him. I can only praise the Good Lord for watching over him and providing the right people in his life (and, prior to her untimely death, for our mother's prayers on his behalf)!

So, once the new venture was up and running, we had this motel with a bus service attached, and my little brother running it all! We went into it with an attitude of, *Let's see where it goes!* It was difficult running the aging motel, but we did the best we could, keeping it at least clean and bug-free, and maintaining low rates. The motel had three small apartments among its rooms, which helped our bottom line, as did the bus station (and the fact that it had a living space for Raymon). One problem developed when Raymon began working a second, part-time job, at the Boone Peddler; the motel position didn't pay very well, and he simply needed pocket money. I was concerned because, with his Peddler job being an evening-only affair, he'd be clocking in over there right around the time people would be looking for motel rooms! Thankfully, he did have someone covering the motel's desk when he was absent, and it was only for a couple nights a week anyway. It all worked out, with Raymon getting the money he needed (and free steak dinners, while helping Bob, too!).

We ran The Longvue in this arrangement for about a year, after which I had the chance to sell it. The price was good and the terms were favorable (I got to hold the mortgage), so I accepted the offer. Raymon kept working at The Peddler, now freed from managing the motel. Meanwhile, I went looking for another investment, and found an apartment building just outside Boone. There I reinvested the motel money, and again moved Raymon in to manage the new property. By this time, in the early '80s, it was over a decade since I'd left Boone for Williamsburg, and I was only getting busier. But, everything was at least stable and moving along, right? Well, that brings us to another twist in my story.

It started with a phone call from Bob Roschy, who was still head honcho at the Boone Peddler. "Dipper," he told me, "I've burned my bridges here in Boone, and I need to leave. Would you and Murray be interested in trading the Myrtle Beach Peddler for mine?" The question left me speechless: the deal would be highly in my and Murray's favor. For starters, we were merely leasing the Myrtle Beach property, whereas the Boone property was *mortgaged*, with only nine years left on the note. Once I got my breath, I said I would confer with Murray and see what he thought—though I could already guess how he would feel! See, Murray had very much wanted to return to Boone someday, and Bob's offer was a prime opportunity to do so. When I told Murray the news, he said he would start packing that day!

We made the exchange, and Murray promptly moved back to Boone as manager. Once the deal was finalized, Murray and I hatched a plan: we would operate the Boone Peddler until we paid it off, then sell it, get real-estate licenses, and go into business in that area. We had the foresight to see that Boone was booming, and what would happen to property values in the town. We could do really well, we decided.

Once more, Charlotte and I were off to the races. We were living in Virginia; the restaurants stayed profitable; my success continued; and now we had a Peddler in Boone. Everything was great, perhaps the best it had ever been—but there was still something *missing* (and we weren't back in Boone). This missing part of me could be sensed but not identified, and it was bringing me down. I felt this lack inside me, but it was also evident elsewhere, in others—including my business partners. They, too, weren't as happy as they used to be, and I think that they sensed my lack of enthusiasm. Bob Roschy, most of all, seemed stricken with this same subtle discontent, as if he too had lost his love of our thriving restaurant enterprise. For me, it was hard to put my finger on what was missing in my life, and I believe that the responsibility of the restaurants and their 150 employees was taking its toll on me. But one thing was for sure: we wanted to return to Boone. Also, I too was worked-out, from my years of going full steam ahead with very few days off. I had another problem, too: we now had a son, Adam, who required my time and attention. All in all, my wonderful life was suddenly underscored with uneasy stirrings—trouble in paradise, you could say.

Soon, that mysterious emptiness and discontent manifested itself, as these things must. The business partnership continued in disharmony until it could no longer be ignored. We had a meeting then, and it didn't go well. We discussed several issues, including the fact that without Charlotte the Super-Hostess working the restaurants, business had declined. Solutions were proposed, then rejected; compromises were refuted similarly; small arguments erupted; egos were piqued. In the end, that business meeting was

45

my last, for I was no longer a partner! There was an upside, however: I was now free to return to Boone!

In hindsight, I see that my leaving the partnership was a good thing. For over ten years I'd been responsible for everything, and now that burden was suddenly lifted off my shoulders. Despite it meaning a financial downturn for me and my family, this twist in the road was ultimately for the best. Afterward, I looked forward to the future and what it might bring.

* * *

By now, it was well over a decade since I'd left Boone for Williamsburg, and we'd traded for the Boone Peddler, bought and sold The Longvue motel, and reinvested in the apartment complex that Raymon was running.

So, once all that was taken care of, I finally moved my family back to Boone.

There, the first order of business was to buy a house, which ended up being a cute A-frame just a few miles from town (Charlotte loved it!). Next, I traded in my flashy Porsche for a more practical vehicle: a Toyota pickup truck. Similarly, my tailor-made suits were replaced by blue jeans. Practicalities aside, these changes reflected an inner shift on my part, one which was ultimately positive—I was back on Earth, my feet returned firmly to the ground, you could say. I had achieved the things I could only dream of while living in the hole outside the football stadium, 15 years earlier—the cars, the positions, the money, the success and all that comes from such a flashy lifestyle. Of course, all of these things would eventually come up short, for material wealth is only a temporary fix and true contentment only comes from the Lord, as I would later learn. But for the time being, at least, life was okay. Murray continued running our Peddler, and Raymon the apartment complex. Things were settling down—including me.

My first month back in Boone, I took it easy, doing little more than enjoying the house that Charlotte and I had bought. Once squared away in that respect, I spent that whole month with my wife and Adam, our young son—such a great little boy, a real gift. I did, however, take the time for one piece of business: I had to foreclose on The Longvue motel, because the new owner just couldn't make it work (after all, he didn't have Raymon!). The good news was that I was able to quickly sell it again, while still carrying the mortgage note. Thankfully, I stopped there and continued my hiatus.

I liked my month off so much, I took a second one. But by the third, I had to get back at it; I just wasn't made to sit around. Coincidentally, just as I was deciding what to do with myself, I got a call from my former Peddler partners, who wanted me to take a couple of restaurants off their hands—perfect timing! The restaurants in question were the Richmond

Peddler and one of the Williamsburg locations. According to them, things weren't going well, and they just wanted to get rid of the places. So off I went to Virginia, where I found someone to take over the Richmond Peddler, and then reopened the other one anew, rebranding it as The Canterbury Tales. Charlotte, however, stayed in Boone, and therein lay the problem, for things just didn't work without her invaluable presence as hostess. To revive the restaurants, it was necessary to bring Charlotte back to Virginia. So she and Adam made the trip, and, like magic, the restaurants did indeed revive.

It was while Charlotte was in Williamsburg that I did something regrettable: I sold our beloved A-frame house in Boone, including its contents—*without telling her*! She was unhappy upon learning of this, to say the least, and it caused a rift in our relationship. Additionally, Charlotte's parents had just recently moved to Boone to be nearer to our family, and so when we didn't return from Virginia, they had to move right back. As an apology, I promised to get rid of the Virginia restaurants and return us to Boone ASAP. Unfortunately, it took a year and a half to find buyers and make good on my promise. But after that, we were, at long last, on our way back south.

Once in Boone, we used the restaurant money to buy a new house: an unfinished cabin on the Watauga River, in a community several miles outside of town. I took it upon myself to finish the place, and my high-school shop classes were suddenly paying off. The cabin took a couple months, and it came out nicely, a neat little place. Charlotte seemed happy again, and so was I. Things had again settled down, it seemed.

However, this calm was short-lived.

Like several times past, my life was shaken up by a phone call: now from the fellow I'd sold the Richmond Peddler to, telling me he was surrendering the property and leaving the place—at the end of the week! The restaurant was, out of nowhere, back on my shoulders. My name was on the lease, and on the equipment payments. A nightmare. I had no choice but to return to Virginia. I got a motel room and, begrudgingly, the keys to the restaurant. I found the operation in disarray; the previous operator had not done well, and most of the customer base was lost. On top of it all, I was running low on cash. I had to find another buyer, and fast, but there was no interest when I advertised the property. Circumstances had conspired against me.

In the meantime, I was running the Richmond Peddler almost entirely by myself. I would literally take an order, go next door to a supermarket for the food, then cook it—talk about stress! I couldn't keep going that way. On a Tuesday afternoon, I decided that if I didn't sell the place by Saturday, I would have to close it down and move back to Boone, after which I could expect to be sued for the lease and equipment. But, thankfully, it didn't come to that, for I soon got a bite on the restaurant.

The man sounded highly interested; he wanted to see the place the next day. It revived me somewhat—I had one more chance! When I met the prospective buyer the following afternoon, he seemed pleasant, and as interested as he'd sounded over the phone. I gave him a tour of the facilities, and we were soon discussing a figure. Before the man committed to anything, however, he decided to take one more look around. While browsing the kitchen, he asked to go inside the walk-in cooler—which I'd been hoping he would neglect. See, where the cooler would've normally been filled, it currently contained only one onion—literally one single onion, sitting all by its lonesome on a shelf (it was, at least, a big onion). The sight didn't speak well of the business.

The man looked all around the cooler, taking in the emptiness. A silence unfolded. Then he said, "You must've been really busy. All your food is gone." I nodded, and said: "Very!"

The sale was a go, and we agreed on a price of $75,000, with $50,000 immediately and then the rest after six months. But there was a catch: the new owner had little interest in the restaurant business. It was, I would learn, a repeat of the St. Louis doughnut shop: the Richmond Peddler was to become a mob front. The man explained to me how he was in the Mafia, and that the purchase would be along those lines. As for the sale, the man would have to go to New York and get the money from his godfather. "I'll meet you back here on Saturday at three," he finished. I didn't know what to say; though, really, I had no choice but accept. I had nothing to lose, since I was leaving Saturday anyhow, one way or another. "Okay," I said, and that was that.

The next three days were gut-wrenching. Nightmarish outcomes filled my thoughts, and Saturday felt to be years away. The mafioso gentleman had, at least, agreed to take over the lease and equipment payments immediately, and that helped in itself. On Saturday at 3:00 PM, I was in my Toyota pickup truck, waiting in the parking lot behind the business, counting the minutes—when in pulls a long black car. My heart almost stopped. Out stepped my buyer, a brown paper bag in his hands. He gave me the bag and said, "I hope you don't mind that it's all in fives, tens, and twenties. My godfather owns a bunch of pizza restaurants." I accepted the bag without hesitation, telling him that fives, tens, and twenties were fine. We shook hands. I returned to my truck. "See you in six months," I said in parting, and I immediately left for Boone.

The relief was beyond words. I couldn't believe I'd been delivered of the restaurant. That drive back to Boone was my best ever. I couldn't wait to see Charlotte and my little boy. When I told her the story of the sale, Charlotte was awestruck, too. What had looked hopeless was now a great blessing. After that, I was out of the restaurant business (except for the Boone Peddler, which was still

48

being run by Murray Broome), and I never looked back. Once again, I was hopeful for the future, and couldn't wait to see what was next.

Select Pictures

Me with my friends in early high school (I am second from left)

Picture that appeared in my hometown newspaper, under the headline
"Dipper Scores 28 Points—Big Win For Millville High"

The motorcycle I would crash in a head-on collision

The college dead-lifting competition I would win, soon before breaking the
NC dead-lifting record

College graduation

My wedding to Charlotte (my brother, Raymon, is at the far right)

Charlotte and her mother, Pearl

A recent picture of myself

My sons, Adam (left) and Aaron, circa 1989

The Peddler of Boone, which I would wash dishes at, then own

The Peddler of North Myrtle Beach, which Murray Broome and I would trade to Bob Roschy for the Boone property in a windfall deal

The Peddler of Newport News, VA

The Longvue Motel

The A-frame house that I would sell without informing Charlotte

The mountaintop dream house that Cam Perry and I built for Charlotte

The sensational view from that property, which would entice me into purchasing it

My "vice car," purchased wholly with money that would've otherwise gone to drinking and partying

The fiberglass Corvette that was utterly destroyed after I fell asleep at the wheel and drove it into the woods

For more than 20 years, motel owner Floyd "Dipper" Garrison has owned the Elk Motel on the outskirts of Boone.

Marie Freeman
Watauga Democrat

THE ELK MOTEL & DIPPER'S REDEMPTION

The front-page newspaper article detailing my campaign to save The Elk Motel

Floyd and Charlotte Garrison, 2015

Chapter XI: Back to Boone, and More Surprises

By this point in my life, it had been twelve years since that fateful night when I washed dishes for Bob Roschy at the Boone Peddler. Much had happened in that time, but my life story still had plenty of upcoming chapters, and plenty of surprises in store.

My housing situation was the next change to come about. When I returned to Boone after unloading the Richmond Peddler to the mob, in 1981, I got an offer from someone looking to buy the riverside cabin that my family and I were living in. The offer was reasonable, and I still wanted to build my wife her dream home; so the sale went through. When it came to the dream home, however, those plans weren't as grand as they used to seem. See, Charlotte's priorities had shifted.

After years of our stressful, nonstop lifestyle, my wife had changed her mind about pursuing a house and being a stay-at-home mom. With my constantly being either away or at work (or *burdened* by thoughts of work), she'd decided that the price of success wasn't worth it. But I was oblivious to her new attitude (man is so much in the dark, unseeing, unhearing). She'd tried to tell me—to forget building the house, that she was willing to keep working if she had to, even after kids, because she just wanted her husband back and a quiet life—but I was just too far away, lost in myself and my work and my problems. As it so happened, the Richmond debacle had been the last straw for her, with my having to flee Boone and abandon my wife and child at short notice. Yet, for all her attempts to communicate, I still didn't get it. So I sold our cabin and went forward with the dream house that Charlotte had decided was no longer worth the craziness it entailed.

I found a little house for sale, and this one was also comfortably outside of town, a few miles farther down the Watauga River. It needed some work, but it came with close to 20 acres of land, plus a nice big barn (and a chicken coop!). Best of all, there was a separate, one-acre lot, overlooking the Watauga River from the very top of the property, that would be perfect for Charlotte's dream house—sold! With that, I was the proud owner of the ideal backdrop for my family's future (or so I thought), and while I set to work on the new property's preexisting house, we moved into a townhouse in Boone, under the idea that we would then move into the other house once renovations were complete. It was then that we were blessed with the conception of our second son, Aaron; and, luckily, the new house's renovations were done in time for us to move from the townhouse prior to his birth, in the summer of 1983. After that, I built a log cabin on the property, right behind the barn, with some hundred-year-old logs that I'd bought cheap (found in another barn, ironically). I then moved our four-strong family into *there*, and sold off the first house. We were rather migrant at that time.

I enjoyed building and selling homes, I found then; it was the perfect profession for me. By the time we were living in that latest log house, I was really into the whole construction thing, and fully ready to start on my next project (the dream house). But, before that could happen, I was once again summoned to Richmond, VA.

At this point, it was six months since I'd unloaded the Richmond Peddler to the mafioso gentleman, which meant it was time for me to be paid the final $25,000 from the sale. So I drove up there, and everything appeared well, with plenty of customers at the retooled restaurant. The man I'd sold it to wasn't there that day, but the restaurant's manager was able to direct me to a pizza place downtown, where I did indeed find the man who owed me the money. I said hello, then told him I was there to pick up the balance on the restaurant, as we'd agreed. And that's where things went wrong: the man looked me straight in the eye and said, "I'm not paying you." When he didn't say anything more, I asked him why he wasn't paying—had I done something wrong, was there something he hadn't received? "No," he answered. "I'm just not paying you!"

Bad as this was, I did have recourse: I still owned the equipment, technically, so I could take it back—good luck running a restaurant without *that*. When I told the man this, he made no response. However, as I turned to walk out, I heard behind me the unmistakable click of a gun being cocked—multiple guns, in fact (the man had friends). I kept walking to the door (well, maybe I was jogging by then), and they didn't shoot; it was daytime and there were people around, and this is the only reason I can think of for them sparing my life (other than God's protection, of course).

Despite my close call, I made good on my promise to reclaim the restaurant equipment. When I got there and started preparations to do so, however, I was met by the manager I'd talked to earlier, who I explained the situation to. Afterward, he sat me down and said that he knew the owner's godfather (from up in New York, who'd paid me the $50,000 in small bills from his pizza restaurants), and that he, the manager, would call the godfather up. So I had a cup of coffee while the manager went to a phone. I didn't know what to think—was the phone call just a ruse, to keep me there until they could come knock me off? After talking on the phone, the manager came back and asked me some questions. When asked if I was owed $25,000, I said yes.

"Come back next Saturday and I'll have your money for you," I was told then. The manager and I shook hands, and I left. When I returned the following Saturday, the same man was there, and he gave me $25,000 in cash! But that's not all: I eventually became friends with the manager, and sold him a large amount of equipment that I'd amassed after my years in the restaurant business. Only God could orchestrate such a story!

Chapter XII: Another Man is a Game-Changer for Me

After my run-in with the mob, I was at last free to build Charlotte's dream house (whether she wanted it or not). It was 1985, long after the home's conception, but it finally got going.

This one was to be another log house, so I went looking for logs like those I'd used to build the house beyond the property's barn. Such logs were hard to find, but I was able to secure some more. Next, I decided I needed a dump truck and a bulldozer, since it looked like I was going to keep building for a living. I'd seen a good dozer two years earlier (a 450 with a four-in-one front bucket and a backhoe in the back—perfect!), and had told the owner to call me if he ever decided to sell it. The man's name was Cam Perry, and every subsequent time I saw him, he still didn't want to sell. Well, right around when I needed the dozer, I saw Cam's truck sitting in a parking lot in Boone, so I pulled over and waited for him there. This time when asked if he was ready to sell, Cam looked at me with a smile and said yes! I almost jumped out of my boots, it was such great news. He sold me the dozer, paired with a great dump truck and a trailer—I was in love!

I didn't realize it at the time, but when I bought Cam Perry's dozer, I was getting *him* too!

The Good Lord was still answering my dear mother's prayers, and Cam was a part of those answers! God had placed many people in my life along the way, but Cam was like no other—what a gift from Heaven! We got to know one another, then started doing odd jobs together in an informal little business, and that's how I would hear his story. Cam was in his early 50s when I met him, and I learned that he'd been on the operating table at 43, with all kinds of lines and tubes going into him. It hadn't looked like he was going to make it; they'd thought he would be dead by the next day. Back then, Cam had wanted nothing to do with religion or God, and hadn't had a very good life. But that night after his operation, he called out to God and asked to be saved and healed—and he walked out of the hospital a few days later, a new man. Cam was one of the first people I ever met who showed me Jesus, and who truly lived the Christian life.

Before Cam, the only true Christian men I'd met were Dr. Davies, who had saved my leg after my motorcycle accident; Jack Howell, who gave me my first hardware-store job; and Leon Spencer, a neighbor from my youth. Despite these encounters, I had always thought that Christian men were mostly wimps; several of those I'd known just hadn't come across as "real" men. To me, taking a humble, turn-the-other-cheek attitude didn't seem to be very mannish behavior. However, that perception would change, while I was in school getting my graduate degree.

It happened back when I was in charge of the college weight room. One day the athletic director told me I needed to set up ten exercise stations around the campus, because a man named Paul Anderson was arriving the next day, to put on an exhibition. I didn't know the name at the time, but Anderson was, then, the strongest man in the world—a 6'1", 350-pound monster of a man. When he arrived, 2,000 people showed up to see him. I'd set up the stations all around campus as asked, and the first was a chair with two 250-pound dumbbells. Casually, Anderson picked them up and began pumping them while telling us about his life, as easily as if he were washing dishes. At one of the other stations, several audience members boarded a broad platform—which Anderson then lifted up! Wow! I was astounded, like everyone else. Finally, we came to the school library, and not a single person had left the crowd. There, Anderson took a penny out of his pocket, threw it on the grass, and then, as he went to retrieve it, said, "I'm the strongest man in the world, but without Jesus Christ I can't even pick up this penny." What a game-changer *that* was! I was later introduced to him, and we spent some time talking. What an amazing man. You'd never believe that he was once a 98-pound weakling. (His remarkable story is told in the book *Paul Anderson: The Mightiest Minister*).

Paul Anderson, a "real" man, changed my view of Christian men, as did Cam Perry, with his true heart for Jesus. Later, Cam told me that the only reason he'd sold me his prized bulldozer was because God had told him to! Of course, I didn't understand it all at the time (that God has a plan, and orchestrates things to fulfill that plan), but we don't have to understand something for it to work. Thank God for that!

* * *

So, back to Charlotte's dream house.

Now that I had my land, my logs, and my equipment, I was ready to begin construction. First, however, I would get interrupted by yet another phone call.

Right away, I knew it was one of "those" calls, the kind that nobody wants (those which would often see me spontaneously leaving town). This time, the caller was the man who'd bought The Longvue Motel the second time I'd sold it, informing me that he couldn't make his payment and, therefore, was surrendering the place—returning that burden squarely to my shoulders. Sounds familiar. At least I'd gotten a down payment from him, so the deal hadn't been a total waste of time. And, thankfully, I did find another buyer shortly afterward, allowing me to sell The Longvue for a third time. This latest buyer seemed confident that he could make it work, and because I lived in hope, I let him do his thing.

After that, I once again set upon beginning the dream house (while studying for the real-estate test, as Murray and I had planned several years prior), and this time—praise the Lord!—I actually managed to get started. Here, Cam Perry returns to the stage of my life, for he was just the partner I needed when constructing the new house. Cam could do it all: carpenter, block mason, equipment operator, all-around handyman. Plus, he *taught me* these things. On top of all that, Cam had integrity and was dependable, someone I could count on. He was a big encouragement in general, and his help was invaluable.

Even before completing the dream house, I was looking to the future, already thinking about building another log house, as a rental, once my own was done. I had already bought a couple rental homes that came with enough land for more construction, and so this upcoming house, I decided, would go on one of those properties. It was an expansive period for me. Unfortunately, right when I was making these plans, *Southern Living* magazine ran an article about building a home using "old logs," so the market for the logs I favored suddenly blew up, inflating the price sky-high—there went my other log house. But, no sooner had that possibility evaporated than a new one was laid at my feet.

As luck would have it, a man offered to give me a house; all I had to do was move it away. *A free house*, are you kidding me?! This would've been a big deal anytime, but then, in Boone, it was unheard of. See, Boone was rapidly growing at the time, having been "discovered." The school had gone from a 3,200-student teachers' college to a 10,000-strong university; Floridian tourists were flocking to town; a real-estate bubble had formed; the state government was promoting further growth by promising to run four-lane highways to the area—all of which contributed to a need for housing, with even low-rent accommodations in large demand. So, you can imagine that being offered a house at moving cost was music to my ears. Talk about being in the right place at the right time!

Working on the dream home on the side, I started looking for a house-moving company, which led me about thirty miles from Boone, to West Jefferson, NC, and a man named David Bare. The outfit was a father-and-son team with a small crew of workers, and after assessing the free house, they quoted the very reasonable price of $4,000 to move it to one of my lots. More music to my ears. Cam liked the idea, too, and was willing to do the foundation and other work. The sale was a go, and the move went without a hitch, with the house fitting perfectly on Cam's foundation. So, within just a few weeks, I was the proud new owner of another rental house. After the moving costs, the land, and some minor work on the home, I had $7,500 in a $40,000, ready-to-rent property. Great! These sort of deals would prove to be typical for me, in another demonstration of God's hand in my life.

And still my property business grew. No sooner had I finished with the all-but-free house than I got a phone call from a customer I'd had at the Williamsburg Peddler, a guy known for being into real estate. He had a new deal for me: a prefab house that he'd intended to put up as model (after importing it from Finland, where the man knew a magistrate). Unfortunately for my friend, the Virginia state government wouldn't grant him the necessary permits for the house; but, he said, North Carolina would. There were several of these houses available, he explained, and they could be stacked and made into apartment buildings, side by side, like a strip mall. These curious Finnish homes were shipped two to a 40-foot container, and included everything, right down to the proverbial kitchen sink. Structurally, they came in Lego-like 4'-by-8' sections, with doors and windows already installed. Just fasten the sections together, and instant house! Once its foundation was finished, a house could be completed in as little as three days. The homes were unbelievably great, way ahead of their time. To me, they appeared to be the solution to the world's housing problems.

The best part was, there were 2,000 of these units, and they were *cheap*. My friend explained the situation to me. The houses had been constructed by the socialist-leaning Finnish government, at a plant where the guys in charge had a scheme going: they would run off a few extras when they had a large order, then tuck them away before selling them on the side. The Finnish magistrate, my friend said, had found the 2,000 homes illegally stored in a warehouse, after which the magistrate had promptly replaced the warehouse's locks with his own, then notified the plant workers that the houses had been seized. Now, trying to offload them, the Finnish magistrate had contacted my friend with the deal of a lifetime: a container of two homes, shipped anywhere on the East Coast, *for $5,000 each*—$2,500 a house! Incredible!

Upon hearing all this, I had to curb my enthusiasm, for it sounded too good to be true. And besides, my plate was pretty full already, with my moving houses while staying busy with Charlotte's dream home. So I put the deal off, interested but not ready to make a commitment. My real-estate friend kept calling, however, and he finally told me that he had to take down his unpermitted model, and that I'd better come and get it if I was really interested. That was a Wednesday, and by Saturday Cam, my brother, and I were in Williamsburg with a dump truck and a trailer. As we pulled up, I was speechless: the model was even *better* than my friend had described. The three of us took it apart and loaded it up, and then, $2,500 lighter, we set off for Boone with a Finnish prefab home. With Cam's wisdom, I decided to put the house on a block foundation and make it a duplex, which went well (Cam supplied this foundation, too). It went so well, in fact, I envisioned buying 200 more of these babies and planting them around Boone like seeds, and then maybe some more for Myrtle Beach—talk about excited! I thought these prefab homes were the best thing ever!

However, my grand vision would not pan out. When I called my real-estate friend to put in the first order for more houses from his Finnish connection, he informed me that I'd waited too long—they were sold out! It had been six months since he'd originally called; my hesitation had cost me the deal. It was another *Wow!* moment, now in the negative. I was a little heartbroken, but at least I did have my one unit (and the right to say that I owned a house imported from Finland).

Really, it might've been a good thing that the Finnish-house plan fell through, because otherwise I might *never* have completed Charlotte's dream home. But complete it I did, and she loved it (or so it seemed).

Chapter XIII: A Bomb is Dropped

Despite appearing to live the good life, I was about to have a bomb dropped on me, and I didn't have a clue! Warning signs were all around me, I just didn't see them. This time, the problem was not in my business life, but in my own home.

It began one day in 1989, when I came home to have lunch, shortly after completion of the dream house.

I was so happy. I'd just finished moving into a beautiful new home; I had two wonderful sons; Cam was a great help; I was staying busy with my properties; The Peddler was doing great, with Murray Broome managing it (and soon it would be paid off)—the good life indeed. Though I was still going a hundred miles an hour, working nonstop, I was thrilled at all that had happened since I'd gotten married and then washed dishes that fateful night at the restaurant. These were my thoughts as I parked my truck and walked down the driveway to the dream house. That's when I noticed Charlotte, standing on the deck with a look on her face that I'd never seen before. Next, she said the words I never imagined I would hear: "I don't love you anymore. I want you to pack your bags and leave!"

There goes the bomb—*kaboom*! I was in shock, to put it mildly. I couldn't comprehend what she had just said. It was a nightmare in every sense, and I wanted to wake up!

I remember continuing on into the house and then packing a suitcase. I came back out, and when Charlotte didn't say anything more, I returned to my truck and keyed the ignition. Only as I started backing out did I come to my senses. "What are you doing?" I said to myself. "That's your wife and children in there! This is your home!" I looked back, and Charlotte was still standing on the deck, now with a smile on her face. When I stopped the truck and came back out, her smile turned into a look of horror. "This is my house," I told her. "I'm not going anywhere." She got angry then, and, having never seen her like this before, I didn't know what was going on, or why. She still wouldn't speak, and I didn't know what to say. That was a long day, and a longer night.

All the while, I was trying to think what I might have done to arouse this in Charlotte. I'd sold her beloved A-frame house without telling her, causing her parents to move back to New Jersey; and there were all those times I'd gone away for weeks on end due to work and the restaurants, often leaving in the middle of the night. Surely this had put a strain on things, and some distance between myself and my family (though I'd had no choice in these matters, and I'd done it all *for* Charlotte). Plus, just the week before she'd told me to leave, I'd made another mistake: just as Charlotte had finished serving me a big meal, then finally sat herself down to eat, I'd ordered her to get me some ketchup, not too politely. (Ketchup was always getting me into trouble—remember Pam's parents?) It might not sound like such a crime, but with everything building up the way it was, the incident was blown out of proportion. You should've seen the look on her face; it reminded me of when I'd sold the A-frame house! She'd fetched me the ketchup, slammed it down, then stormed out the back door, not saying a word the rest of the night—it must've been the last straw, that which broke the camel's back.

She'd tried to discuss these problems with me, of course; but, with me being so preoccupied with work (if not absent completely), it had all gone in one ear and out the other. Only after the fact, when it was too late, did I see it all from her standpoint: how I'd neglected her for all these years, and taken her for granted, and always insisted on being taken care of whenever I was home. What an eye-opener!

The next couple weeks after she'd told me to leave, I tried to get through to her, but it was like talking to a brick wall. I kept hoping that this nightmare would end, that I would wake up and have it all be over; but no such luck. As it so happened, I did have some waking up to do, but it was bigger than a mere impolite order for ketchup. It all hit me at once: I'd been mistreating the woman who was my wife, the mother of my children, the sweetest, most caring, giving, unselfish, loving person I had ever met. I'd unknowingly driven her over the edge, and she was now in big trouble, emotionally and mentally. Simultaneously, I had another awakening: that I'd fallen away from the Lord. After growing up in the loving hands of my Christian mother, going to church and believing in God, I'd been leading my adult life completely in the other direction, and it all stemmed from my anger at Him for allowing my mother to die at the age of 36!

It was a huge reality check for me. I'd sensed something wrong before, from that vague emptiness inside me, but that hadn't been clear enough to show me what was really going on. It would take my marital problems to wake me up to myself, acting as a catalyst—and was my awakening ever a rude one. Another thing that came to me then: not only had I neglected to surrender my life to God, I didn't even *know* Him in the first place! Sure, I believed in "God," but only in an abstract way, not as an actual, living being. I recall thinking that, after giving up my vices and getting married, I'd become a pretty good person—balancing the scales, as it were, to "more good than bad." And, since I believed in God, I thought I was okay and could claim to be a Christian—wrong! How blind I was: even though God had provided many, many signs—from sending Christian men into my life, to intervening in my many near-death experiences—my knowledge of Him had remained the stunted, childish notions that I shared with much of the secular world. After all, even Satan believes in God; he's just in rebellion, not going to surrender, and will always stay in that state.

These understandings about my spiritual status were another shock, maybe the biggest of all. But once they sunk in—I got it! Boy, you talk about being blind, deaf, and stubborn—I was it, and I hadn't a clue! The night that I finally awakened to all this, I stumbled out of the house, fell on my knees, and cried out to God to forgive me for all that I'd done (or not done), tears rolling down my cheeks. I asked God to help me with my wife, to please, *please* heal this marriage! With that, I surrendered my life to Jesus Christ, and my dear mother's prayers for salvation were at last answered!

Afterward, I went back inside the house, not knowing exactly what had just happened. Nor did I know that my life was about to change, and radically. I knew one thing, though: I'd meant what I said to God. Also, I knew I was at the end of my rope, and that if God didn't intervene, life as I knew it was over! Thankfully, intervention would come, and fast, by the very next morning.

That night, I had a real hard time getting to sleep (especially with Charlotte sleeping separately from me, as she'd begun doing after our problems started). But by the next morning, I was a different person, and I knew it. I didn't *understand* what had occurred, exactly, but the sense of change was no less felt. I remember jumping out of bed, running to the bathroom, and looking into the mirror, expecting to see some alien creature staring back at me; to my relief, there was only the same old me. Except, as I stood there looking in the mirror, I heard a voice: "I've changed you on the *inside*, not the outside," it said, laughing. It was God, I knew, though I still didn't really understand what was happening. When it comes to this sort of thing, I don't think it's really possible to explain.

My transformation still amazes me to this day; though, not everyone was so impressed. I remember hearing Charlotte, on the phone, say that Dipper was acting like a different person. "But I know he's the same old Dip," she added. My transformation was all a ruse, she decided, and there was no helping things. Of course, she hadn't a clue of what had happened inside me; and besides, my dear wife wasn't the devout Christian she'd made herself out to be. Yes, my sweet, wonderful, choir-singing, church-going Charlotte was a Christian in name only! She was in the same boat I'd been in: only knowing God in an empty, superficial way! Like the old me, she had no idea what a born-again believer was. So it was only natural that she distrust my change.

But I didn't let it bring me down. Instead, I kept praying, and believing that God would melt her hard heart and restore our marriage. Though, even before that could happen, I was surprised to find myself at peace, and feeling joy in the face of our horrible situation. That I could feel anything approaching happiness throughout this mess (which was, on top of everything else, impacting my sons), is testimony to the power of God. I also found a new reserve of patience, which certainly came in handy. The Lord had mercy on me, I suppose.

Indeed, that saintly patience was most necessary over the next six months, for little changed on Charlotte's end, and she kept trying to get rid of me. Likewise, I kept praying for God to repair my marriage and give me my wife back, refusing to give up. To God, I probably sounded like a broken record, praying again and again in the face of what looked to be a hopeless situation. My doggedness wasn't all good, though, for I was doing all the talking, not stopping to listen to God. Eventually, one day when I was repeating my same prayers, God interrupted me: "When you want Me like you want your marriage fixed," He said, "then we'll begin the work that needs to be done!"

It brought about another realization: I'd been focusing on the wrong things, thinking the problem was all in my marriage, not with God—putting the cart before the horse. Get right with God, and the marriage would follow, not the other way around. Realizing my mistake, I apologized to the Lord for putting my marriage ahead of Him, and that day, I decided that God would always be the most important thing in my life (whether He healed my marriage or not). He was all I needed and His love would always be sufficient, whatever happened in my marriage. I would always be grateful, I told God. Also, I offered to trade my salvation in exchange for that of my wife—I would go to Hell for her, I told God. Of course, I didn't yet know that it doesn't work that way, for each and every person must achieve their *own* salvation (just like you can't eat someone else's meals for them).

After making this pledge, I dove into my Bible, learning about this God that had rescued me. Then, I was even thirstier to know Him than before. I would often have Christian radio playing, with the TV on a Christian station, and a Bible open on my lap—I couldn't get enough. For sure, I had started listening to, more than talking to, God. It was what He wanted, and what I *needed*! As for Charlotte, my new studies drove her crazy. Here I was, with my marriage falling apart, about to lose everything I'd worked for, and all I can do is go around telling people about this Jesus I'd found. I just couldn't stop—and I *still* can't stop! (It's one reason I wrote this book!)

Yet my marriage stayed broken. And to make things worse, the people in my life were tired of hearing about my and Charlotte's problems. Even our pastor was indicating that we should throw in the towel, that our marriage was hopeless and that I should move on. Our support dried up, and it pushed us that much closer to the unspeakable: divorce. Eventually, there came a time when only two people continued encouraging us: Cam Perry, and a family friend named Doris, both of whom had faith that all things are possible with God. They didn't give up on Charlotte, and thank God for them! I know that God placed them in our lives for this very purpose, to help Charlotte and me through our marital storm. Their faith was great— what blessings they were!

However, time and fatigue would take their toll. Once it had been almost a year since Charlotte's asking me to leave, even *I* was struggling to persevere in my faith that our marriage could be healed. But then, one day when I was almost ready to give up, I ran into Ms. Doris at the supermarket. Seeing that I was down, she told me that God was at work and to trust in Him—and then she prayed for me, right there by the deli. It worked to prop up my ailing faith, and that night, I was further encouraged when I came to another important realization. "If your wife had cancer," God asked me then, "what would you do?" I answered, "Whatever I would have to, and I'd never stop trying to get her healed!" Next He said, "Your wife has cancer, but it's of a spiritual and mental kind, not physical." I understood what God was getting at: hang in there and do what I had to do, no matter what. It really put things into perspective.

God's encouragement didn't stop there. The day after Doris prayed for me at the supermarket, I got a call that I had a broken pipe at the motel (yes, The Longvue, which I had *again* come into possession of, for the third and final time). I called several plumbers but none could come, so I went to the Yellow Pages, which led me to a plumber named Steve. Unfortunately, this man, also, was out on a job and couldn't immediately come to the motel, and there was no one else. Sixteen rooms without water—what was I going to do?! Well, I prayed, and the next thing I knew, there was Steve the plumber, pulling up at the motel. He said to me, "I don't know why I'm here, but I know it involves more than a broken pipe. Let me fix the pipe first, then we'll talk!" I didn't know what to make of this; I'd never seen this man before (Steve was one of the few people in Boone I didn't know). But, so long as he fixed the pipe, I would talk with him all he wanted.

Once finished with the repairs on the motel, Steve came to me and said, "Okay, it's fixed. Now, what else is going on?" Without hesitation, I told him that my marriage was on the rocks. "So is mine," Steve replied, and then proceeded to tell me the story of how, several years previously, his wife had just broken down and withdrawn from him and his kids. She'd continued living in the same house, but had nothing to do with her family, and Steve had had no idea what was wrong or what had caused it to happen. Consequently, he would have to get up at 4:30 AM to prepare for the day, doing all the cooking, cleaning, and housework, plus getting the kids ready for school and packing their lunches, all before working hard all day long and then returning home for more of the same. Meanwhile, his wife would simply get up and go to work! This had gone on for years, without breaks, and when I asked Steve how long he planned to keep it up, he told me: "Dipper, I'm a Christian, and when I took my wedding vows, it was for better or worse and for as long as I live. So, how long? For the rest of my life, I guess, because by faith, I'm never going to give up!" After Steve left me that day, I thought, *If he can do it for all this time, in a situation that's even worse than mine, I can keep going, too!*

(A footnote about Steve the plumber: A couple years later, he called me to report that his wife had come back and his marriage was better than ever. Praise God!)

So I pressed on with my marriage. I remember still trying to love on Charlotte (the Bible says to love your enemies), but things only got harder. One time, I took her flowers, and she threw them down and said, "Don't buy me any flowers! I don't want anything from you!" At Christmas, I bought her the dishwasher she'd always wanted, and even that sent her into a rage—"Just leave!" No matter what I said or did, it made no difference. Finally, she told me that *she* was leaving.

Charlotte was leaving me—a disaster! But, amazingly, things would still get worse. There was another man.

It started with Charlotte's father, Burt, when he had a stroke. Burt still lived in New Jersey (Charlotte's mother, Pearl, had passed away some time before our marital crisis), and Charlotte had been making arrangements for him to get the help he needed. To do this, she'd been writing to some fellow up there, I knew; though, only by chance did I learn the true nature of her pen pal. I was driving near the Boone mall one night, on my way home, when the Holy Spirit impressed upon me to stop there, directing me to the parking area. I had no business at the mall, and no logical reason to follow my urge, yet I found myself turning in, with no idea what was going on— and there, by the entrance, was our family van. Dusk had fallen, and it was dark enough that I could see the van's interior light shining. I thought, *What's going on here?* Suspicious now, I turned off my truck's headlights and then pulled up behind the van. Quietly, I got out and looked into the van, and there was Charlotte, alone, reading a letter. I opened the van and, to Charlotte's surprise, grabbed the letter—which turned out to be a love letter from New Jersey!

It sealed the deal on her leaving me, and it appeared our marriage was truly over—but I wasn't through yet. The day after I discovered her in the van, I went to my lawyer and had him draw up some papers that I hoped would change her mind: a legal declaration that, were she to leave me, she would surrender all rights to our businesses and homes, including all money and cars, and custody of our sons. She had threatened to leave before, but when I'd told her she'd go with nothing, it would change her mind. So I thought the papers would stop her again. But they didn't this time, for she signed them. Her only demand was that I take her to the bus station, where she would leave for Jersey.

So, there I was, taking my wife and her two suitcases to a bus station, thinking I would never see her again. My heart was breaking, and tears rolled down my face. The bus carried her away, then I got back in my truck. What a long trip home *that* was. I couldn't imagine going back to our dream house on the mountaintop without Charlotte waiting for me there. Plus, I felt I had failed God by not winning her back. I kept thinking of how He hadn't wanted me to give up, and had continued to encourage me, promising that, so long as I put Him first in my life, He would put things right with my marriage—so why had she *left*? What was I going to do now? Once I got home, my heart stayed broken and my sons missed their mother. I had no idea how the situation would turn out, and this uncertainty didn't help things.

However, God was still at work, as evidenced by an unexpected phone call I got about a week later. To my surprise, it was Charlotte, asking if she could come back. I told her to let me think about it (and pray about it, too)—which was the truth, because I'd told her that if she left, it was final, no changing her mind. I wanted to say yes, as soon as she'd asked to come back, but I had promised the Lord that I would consult with Him before any major decisions. So I got down next to our bed, on my knees, and asked God what to do. I got an answer immediately: "Yes, take her back, go get her—*now!*" But, what about my sons? Well, God solved that problem, too, by providing a caretaker in just minutes.

With that, I called Charlotte back. After seeming to take forever to get through and hear her voice, I told her my answer, and she agreed to take a train back to Boone in a few days. I didn't tell her I was coming to get her.

I left the next afternoon, and got to Jersey in less than a day. I pulled up to her father's house, where she'd fled to, and knocked on the door. Charlotte appeared, and oh! what a look she had, even worse than when I'd sold that troublesome A-frame house (or rudely asked her for ketchup that one night). She asked, "What are you doing here?!" When I replied that I'd come to bring her back home, she said that she wasn't going back with me, she would take the train. I started to comply with her wishes, returning to my truck; except, then I remembered what the Lord had said, to go get her *now*. So I pulled back into the driveway, then went to the door and pleaded with Charlotte to go back with me; but the answer was still no. I then left and returned *again*, for a third try (third time's a charm), now telling her that if she didn't come back with me, not to come at all! She then agreed, but only reluctantly. Later on, I found out that she didn't want to go that day because she'd planned to meet up with her man-friend before leaving town. It explained God's emphatic "*Now!*"

We were back in Boone by the next day, and as bad as things were, I was glad to have her home. The boys needed their mother, for one; also, I again had hope that it wasn't over yet, even though she now seemed worse than before she left. A couple weeks went by like this, and I began thinking I'd made a big mistake bringing her back—and that was before I knew what she was *really* doing at the time. Years afterward, Charlotte told me that she had come up with a plan: she would return home, feign a relationship with me until our sons were grown, and then leave me for good. Her life was a lie, but you wouldn't have known it; after deceiving me repeatedly over the year in which she'd had her affair with the man in New Jersey, she'd gotten pretty good at it. It's probably for the better that I didn't know this until later on, as it might've otherwise been too much to bear.

By this time, it had been over a year and a half since the trouble started, and life had become Hell on earth. Every day, I pled with the Lord for Charlotte's salvation and a new heart for her, and every day I was disappointed. But the Good Lord was still faithful, for I was soon to see my prayers miraculously answered—what surprises were in store for me!

* * *

Before I go on, I should note that this chapter was probably the hardest to write. Just remembering that period of time is still very painful to Charlotte and me, but we also rejoice at what God has done! Also, I want to stress that it was my fault my wife got into trouble in the first place, because there was no excuse for my neglecting her and for the way I made her suffer all those years. Because of my behavior, she came under attack from Satan himself. Through all this, Satan tried to destroy my marriage and my wife, and if God hadn't intervened, the attack might've been successful! So, all the glory belongs to Him! Even now, I continue to praise Him for all that He's done (and still does)!

88

Chapter XIV: Marriage on the Rocks

Overall, my marital troubles taught me two things. One: don't ever give up, because nothing is impossible with God. Two: God may not always do things when you want Him to, but He's always right on time! Both of these truths were evidenced by the miraculous healing of my and Charlotte's marriage.

It began with a strange incident that occurred late one night in 1991, after Charlotte had returned home from New Jersey.

During that time, our sleeping arrangements hadn't changed: I had the master bedroom, upstairs, and Charlotte had a large, longue-type chair, downstairs. So, when the incident occurred on the night in question, I was alone in the upstairs bedroom, asleep. What happened was, at around 4:00 AM, I was awakened by a sweet little voice that I hadn't heard in a long time, calling my name—"Dipper!" It woke me from a deep sleep, disoriented and surprised. I didn't know what was going on, but the voice had my attention, so I ran downstairs. At the bottom of the stairs, I went to put on the light—but there was *already* light, shining from the kitchen nearby. It was as if the sun was out; but it wasn't daytime. Carefully, I rounded the corner into the kitchen.

I couldn't believe what I found there: Charlotte, looking up at me with an angelic expression, tears on her cheeks—and glowing like a light bulb. A wonderful peace came over me as soon as I saw her, and I could tell just by looking at her that all the anger and hostility were gone. "Everything is going to be okay," she told me. "Jesus has touched me, too!" Then she added, "But I can't be an outspoken Christian like you. I can't go telling people about Jesus. I'll have to be a secret-agent sort of Christian." (Charlotte was a somewhat shy and introverted person, except when she was hostess at a restaurant.) I was so happy to see her so improved and changed, I didn't argue with her about evangelizing others for Christ—that could come later. At the time, I was just too overjoyed for her salvation— Charlotte had been *restored*, emotionally and mentally, and both she and my marriage were saved! All that night (and for long afterward), I couldn't stop thanking the Lord for what He'd done! Hearing those words from her as she glowed supernaturally in our kitchen, I was about to shoot through the roof!

For the next three days, Charlotte kept that angelic presence (the total opposite of how she'd appeared for well over a year). She kept her glow, and though it wasn't quite to that supernatural level she'd had that night in the kitchen, it was enough to show me that God had touched my wife, and it was all I could ask for. Those three days, we said hardly a word to one another, but we didn't need to; I was just glad to have my wife back. Her heavenly appearance was enough; it filled me with peace, joy, and love! Actually, Charlotte *still* has a bit of that glow to her, especially when she sings in the choir.

Times when I've given my testimony over the years, I'm often asked why God would light up my wife like that. Well, other than the fact that she'd been visited by God (remember what happened to Moses?), I believe it happened because, after a year and a half of lies and deceit, I probably wouldn't have otherwise believed in her transformation. Whatever the reason, I can't deny what I saw, and at the time, I knew, without a doubt, that there was no question of my wife's condition from that night on. So clear was her redemption, I was left totally at peace with the situation. After those three days of silence following her change, she was back to being the loving, caring, sweet wife I knew—except now one who loved the Lord with all her heart! She started speaking again (and hasn't stopped since). And as for her vow to be a closeted, "secret-agent" Christian? Well, much of her time is now spent telling others (often by letter) about this Jesus who touched and healed and transformed her.

Talk about a turnaround. I'll never get over it!

Charlotte's transformation amazed her as much as myself. Besides the sheer miracle of it all, there was the fact that, before, she'd wholly believed she was saved—when she *wasn't*. Even though Charlotte had appeared every bit a Christian, being raised in the church and singing in the choir and believing herself a good person who loved God, *she was lost*, a total unbeliever with no relationship with the Lord. For us, she was the good girl and I was the bad boy, but we had one thing in common: we were both lost! It all goes back to John 3:7: *You must be born again.* Everything else comes up short, and won't get a person into Heaven!

But, thankfully, we both changed our ways and achieved the free gift of salvation. So, as terrible as our year and a half of marital troubles had been, neither of us would trade it for anything, because it's what God used for us to be saved. Since then, we've realized that God allows bad things to happen in order to get our attention. This is especially true the older we get, when it's far harder to surrender fully to the Lord. I haven't seen many elderly people get saved, and it was all the more reason for Charlotte and I to be grateful for all that happened (and for *when* it happened). The fortunate ones are those who come to Him early in their lives. But then, God never said that life would be easy—just the opposite, actually. The Bible tells us that life is a difficult battle, and truer words were never spoken.

Chapter XV: The Longvue Motel

Would you believe that my story still isn't over? God is just that full of surprises!

* * *

Once Charlotte and I had our marriage restored, it was time to move forward. We had a quiet few days after reuniting, allowing us to catch our breath, but then things got busy again, as if a switch had been thrown. Back to work!

My next project started with yet another phone call, in 1991.

This time, it was from the latest owner of The Longvue, that old motel that kept popping in and out of my hands. Predictably, the man told me that he couldn't make his payment, and was leaving town and giving up the motel—so it was all mine, *again*! This had happened twice before, of course, but this latest handover was different, for I was looking for God to show me His new plan for my life, such that I didn't immediately get upset at the news. In the past, it was all about me and what I wanted; but after I'd surrendered to God, it was all about Him and His plans—and rightfully so, since I owed him everything.

As it so happened, when I next resumed ownership of The Longvue Motel, I was, really, beginning God's new plan for my life!

When I first returned to the property, something happened that would be an indicator of all that was to come. The insolvent owner's phone call had come in on a Friday, and it was Monday before I could get to the motel and see what was going on. As I pulled into the parking lot of the U-shaped building, a man came out of a back-corner room, waving his arms. I was surprised—I hadn't known anyone was there! I stopped my truck and got out, and the man walked over and said, "Are you Dipper?" I told him I was, and the man—I'll call him Billy—said that he'd been dropped off at the motel just as the previous owner was getting ready to leave. When Billy had asked about a room, the owner had told him, "Just give me twenty dollars, and you can stay until Dipper comes, then settle up with him." From there, Billy and I began talking.

He was around 40 years old, dirty and unshaven, in a tee shirt and worn-out pants. He didn't look well at all—looked like someone in trouble. I knew how hard it is to tell someone about the Lord when they're down and out, even back then, and so I had a process for such encounters: I would befriend the person, meet their immediate needs, and then let them see Christ in me, after which I would earn the privilege to share the Lord with them. I decided to do this with Billy, and we started talking. Our conversation went back and forth, with Billy rambling on all the while— until I said something about Jesus. Then, everything changed. "Come into my room and I'll tell you the truth about myself," he said then. Once we were in his room, he went to the nightstand and picked up a razor blade. "Just as you drove in," he said, "I was picking up this blade to kill myself."

He then told me his story: how he was a former preacher, married with kids. His church had been down off the mountain, he said, in Lenoir, NC, where he'd been counseling a woman with whom he'd begun an affair. The truth had gotten out, and he'd lost his church, his family, and everything else. By the time he came to The Longvue, his only friend was the person who'd dropped him off, and that was the last that person wanted to do with Billy. Even his mother and sister had written him off. But, according to him, the worst was that he'd failed the Lord!

The pain was so bad, Billy said, that taking his own life seemed the only answer. I remember looking at him and seeing the pain in his face, and my heart broke for this poor soul. I said, "Let's get down at the foot of this bed and pray," and we did, Billy crying and sobbing. Our prayer session seemed to go on for hours. When we at last got up from the floor, I told Billy that if he promised not to take his life, he could stay at the motel and I could help him. He agreed, and I asked for his mother's phone number, which he gave me. I left Billy upset but alive.

What did all this have to do with God's new plan for my life? Everything! See, after interrupting Billy's suicide that night (and doing so in such a remarkably coincidental fashion, which could only be orchestrated by God), I understood that *this was what I was supposed to do from now on*. I was supposed to help people, as God and others had helped me—I finally *got* it!

After counseling Billy at the motel, I drove home to Charlotte and told her at once that I knew what God wanted us to do with our lives. I told her what had happened at the motel, and that I believed that the Lord wanted me to *keep* the place this time, to make into a mission for the down-and-outs, helping them in any way we could while witnessing to them about the Lord. Charlotte's response was that if I believed that was what God wanted me to do, I'd better do it! It was a revelation, I felt. Who knew?

I sent up a prayer that night. *Yes*, I told God, *I'll be obedient to Your will as best I can, but I'll need lots of help from You. Send me all the ones no one else wants—give me the worst of the worst!* And that was that. I had a new purpose in life.

As for Billy the fallen preacher, I called his mother the day after I intervened in his suicide, and told her how broken her son was. "I'll come up there and get him," she said, and the next day, sure enough, Billy's mother and sister showed up at The Longvue to take him home! Billy, however, was only the first such case of someone being helped through the motel. By the end of that week alone, all its sixteen rooms were rented to similar people. Once again, I was off to the races!

* * *

God really does give you what you ask for, and when I'd asked for my motel to be filled with the people whom no one else would (or could) deal with, He certainly obliged—and more. As I said before, I'd learned that sharing Christ with street people is difficult, since hunger and homelessness usually overshadow issues of spirituality. But the motel was an answer to that: I could house and feed people, and it would open the door to sharing my faith.

And that's just what I did. I would take people in, and if they indicated a desire for help (and were willing to work when a job became available), then I'd put them up at the motel and work along with them on the rest. Once they were on their feet, we could begin dealing with their problems—and all The Longvue's residents had their share of problems! I started a weekly Bible study at the motel, and with help from the various acquaintances and contacts I had, we set about making a difference in these people's lives. For some of the tougher cases, I had to get mental or physical help, with which I was assisted by a few Christian doctors I'd known for years, who were a great blessing in this regard. (Amongst these were Drs. Hal Frazier, Gary Pitts, Charlie Sykes, Bob Ellison, and Richard Furman— all Godly men who provided free medical care because of their love and devotion to Christ!) Some of the motel people had to be committed to mental hospitals, others ended up in jail; but like Billy, some made amends with family or spouses and were able to return home. On the other hand, some just didn't make it at all! (Death visited The Longvue more than once.) But, if nothing else, the people all came to know that at least one person loved them—me! And, before they left, they'd know that God loved them, too. In my operating the motel, my overall philosophy was that if one life could be changed, it was all worth it.

For a typical Longvue story, consider a guy named Eddy. This man was 6'3", weighed 250 pounds, and was tough as nails. Though only in his mid thirties, he'd been in many jails, spending about a third of his life incarcerated in some place or another. You could hit him in the head with a two-by-four all day long, and it wouldn't faze him. Needless to say, Eddy could be really hard to deal with! Over the course of his years-long stay at The Longvue, Eddy tried to kill me twice, once with a machete knife, the other time with a shotgun; but I always told Eddy that I loved him and wanted him to have a normal life (he had nobody, no family or friends, and people were generally scared to be around him). I refused to give up on the man, for I'd seen God do so many miracles and change so many lives (including mine!).

I loved Eddy even when it nearly cost me my family.

One afternoon at the motel, he came over to me and said, "I'm stalking your wife. I just watched her at the post office." I knew he was telling the truth, because the last thing Charlotte had told me that morning was of her plans to visit the post office. Eddy then proceeded to tell me what he planned to do to my sons (who were still little boys), none of which was good. Eddy finished with, "Tell me you love me *now!*" I have to admit: upon hearing him say these things, I didn't feel a whole lot of love for Eddy! However, I'd learned that people know when you mean what you say, and I also knew that Eddy's only hope was for someone to truly love him (love is so powerful, as to change lives). So I silently prayed to God to fill me with love for Eddy—and, instantly, it worked! "Eddy," I said to him then, "I love you with all my heart." And it was the truth. The next thing I knew, Eddie was on his knees, curled around my legs and feet, crying like a baby. (He would later tell me it was the first he'd cried since he was four years old.)

Eddy would become a longtime acquaintance of mine, one of the few I had contact with after they'd moved on from the motel. He stayed at The Longvue for about a year, but was constantly creating problems there, so I moved him to a camper trailer on one of my rental properties, at the edge of town. It wasn't too long before I got a call summoning me to the premises—Eddy was having a shootout with the police! By the time I got there, he was safely in the back of a police car. Luckily, no one was killed. In lieu of jail, Eddy was taken across the state line and told never to come back to Boone. He later wrote me a letter that he was heading west, and I didn't hear any more from him for nearly 20 years (during which I never stopped praying for him). At that time, from out of nowhere, I got a phone call from him, telling me he was in town and asking me to come see him. I didn't know what to expect, but when we met, Eddy said that he just wanted to tell me how his life had changed, and to thank me for loving him so—I'm so glad I never gave up on that man! We talked for a little while, and he decided to once more stay in my current motel (not The Longvue, but a similar outfit just down the road from it, The Elk; more on that later). This time, Eddy stayed on for a couple of months, then hitchhiked out of town. I haven't heard from him since.

Besides fulfilling my mission to change at least one life through the motel, Eddy's case brings up another point: the dangers I faced by operating The Longvue. Eddy was one of the more volatile residents, but he wasn't the only one to threaten my family. The threats got to the point that I was forced to basically hide my family for the next 15 years, lest questionable people show up on our doorstep. My wife is still amazed at how you can try with all your heart to help some people, yet they'll want to do you harm. But that's just the way it is, especially when you're dealing with hurting, drinking-and-drugging human beings. Talk about tough love!

* * *

So, that was my motel ministry, and unlike my past ownerships of The Longvue, this time I kept it for many years. Hundreds of people passed through the motel (and its successor, The Elk), and that was just The Longvue, not counting my standalone rental properties and *their* residents, too, whom also tended toward the down-and-out. (At one point, I had 36 rental properties—the result of moving houses around Boone until the property dried up and it was pretty much impossible to move houses anymore.) More or less, nearly all my tenants needed help in some way or another, wherever they lived. Some of the people didn't accept my help, or did but without gratitude; however, these were offset by the many who greatly appreciated my assistance, and that made it all worthwhile.

All in all, I loved running The Longvue, and I loved the folks it touched. There were difficulties and frustrations—and dangers, thanks to the Eddy-types the motel attracted—but none of my efforts were wasted. God doesn't waste anything, after all.

Chapter XVI: Another Motel—Oh No!

Several times in the book, I referred to The Elk, the motel I had after The Longvue. Well, here's the story on that.

     The Longvue, for all its function as a homeless mission of sorts, was still a business, and like any other business, I needed to turn a profit in order to keep it going, if only to pay the loan I had on it. Having lost its bus-and-freight side by this time, the motel was strictly a motel, without the reduction of overhead I'd enjoyed when first running it. The financial burden was, however, lightened partially by having two people buy in as partners: a friend of mine named Steve (not the plumber), and Murray Broome, my colleague from The Peddler. It was a long-term investment on their part, and our agreement was that I could do whatever I wanted with the motel until my partners and I decided to sell. As it so happened, we would wait almost sixteen years for the right time to do so. Then, I got word that the Holiday Inn and the Lowes franchises were interested in The Longvue's neighboring property, which would up my property's value considerably, thus justifying a sale. The plan was, I would keep the motel going until the franchises broke ground; and that's just how it turned out. When it came time to sell, we had no problem finding a buyer and negotiating a comfortable deal. The sale was a bittersweet moment for me: I was sad to have to close The Longvue's doors, but also *relieved*, for the years of running the place had taken their toll on myself as much as the motel. By now, it was time to sell!

     However, I wasn't quite out of the motel business yet. As soon as word got out that The Longvue was to be sold, in 1998, I got a call from a Mr. Pattel, who owned one of Boone's other old motels, The Elk, just down the street from The Longvue. "Dipper," he said to me, "I heard you're selling The Longvue. Come on over, and I'll sell you my motel!" I agreed to meet him, but only reluctantly; just when it looked like I could get some rest, here I was, faced with plunging right back into the motel business. Also, The Elk had double the rooms of The Longvue, plus a duplex apartment in the office building—which meant twice as many people to deal with. But, still, I talked with Mr. Pattel, and he offered me a really great price, and was willing to finance it, too! I was interested, but not yet ready to make a decision. I told Mr. Pattel I'd need to pray about it, and we parted company.

I went home and told Charlotte about The Elk, and she agreed: we needed to do some serious praying, which we did. A small part of me was hoping that the Lord would say no—that rebellious side in everyone, which desires comfort over what we know is right. But the Lord said yes, and there was no doubt that I was to continue the ministry outreach by purchasing The Elk. Thankfully, my convictions had renewed my enthusiasm for the work, and that helped things. So, after accepting Mr. Pattel's offer, I was not only back in the motel business, but I temporarily had *two* motels, owning both The Elk and The Longvue in the meantime before The Longvue's sale went through. It was a bit of a dilemma: I could barely run just the one on my own—how was I going to run *two*? Well, that brings us to a man who would become another running character in the story of my life: Tony.

Early on in my ownership of The Longvue, I realized the need for a full-time maintenance man to live on the premises. I couldn't be there to run things, obviously, and with the residents' perpetual bad behavior, I needed someone to keep law and order, too. For that first year I ran the motel as a mission, I tried to handle the problem in different ways, but nothing worked. When I did at last attempt to hire someone, no "normal" person wanted anything to do with the job (and I couldn't blame them). And so that led to me hiring on Tony, who was himself a longtime resident of the motel, having lived there almost from the start. He had been an alcoholic—a bad one—but no longer. Now sober, with a wife and daughter to support, he needed a job, and being "one of them," Tony knew the ins and outs of The Longvue like no one else—the perfect candidate! I was hesitant to give him any sort of authority or control at the motel, for I knew that that power would probably get abused, but there was no one else, and I just couldn't keep the motel going on my own. So I approached Tony with the job offer, and he accepted.

As I'd thought, having Tony run The Longvue was not ideal, and sometimes I regretted hiring him (he could be so frustrating you could pull your hair out). But Tony was the right man for the job, for better or worse, the same way that a piece of duct tape can help a problem. There were certainly cons to having him on, for he sometimes inflated the rents of some residents, which was equally impressive and troubling; I kept praying that he would one day surrender to the Lord and help people spiritually, too. But, Tony did change during the time I knew him, and he had his advantages, too, very important ones that you just don't see in anyone who hasn't themselves "been there." I ended up keeping Tony on through the remainder of my motel saga, for nearly 25 years, through several seasons of my life. During that in-between time when I owned The Elk along with The

Longvue, Tony even ran both of them, which was impressive, whatever else could be said about the man. The only thing more impressive about him was the many ways he could defraud me and the motels' residents, plus his other shenanigans (and get away with it all!). Tony did the job, though, and I can't help but be thankful for that.

* * *

I could write a whole book filled just with stories from the motels and their many tenants, but I can sum up my adventure in one sentence: it was a real trip. Similarly, I can sum up the residents' problems: alcohol.

It was probably the number-one pitfall, in terms of both damage and in consistency between the people. To illustrate this, consider another motel person, a man I'll call John. He'd been there for eight months, and had always stayed to himself, so that I couldn't seem to reach him. I tried to encourage John, telling him that I really did love him and care about him; but to no avail. Then one afternoon he invited me to his room, which he'd never done before! Once alone with him there, I was told his story.

John's whole upbringing had been on a family farm, until the age of seventeen, when he'd joined the Army. He'd always been a good kid and had never drank alcohol, but once enlisted, he'd been shipped off to the Korean War, where the inevitable happened. The guys in his unit had constantly invited him out for a beer, and John kept turning them down. But one day, he finally gave in and accepted their offer. From then on, John told me, he continued drinking, and by the time he arrived at the motel, decades later, he'd lost his job, his family, and basically everything else in his life—all because of booze! "I'd come here to do something," he told me eventually, "but I haven't been able to do it." In explanation, he opened a drawer and produced a revolver. "If you want to help me," he said then, tears running down his face, "take this gun and put me out of my misery!" I begged him to let me help, just not in the way he'd asked. I stressed that if only he *wanted* to stop drinking, he could, and it would all go from there. John agreed, and I left him to his lonely room.

Multiply this story by the dozens, and you'll see alcohol's effect on the people I ministered to.

John's story is relevant for another reason, too, for it forced me to confront an alcohol-related shortcoming of my own. After leaving John's room that night, I looked across the street from The Longvue, to The Peddler Steakhouse, which I still owned interests in—and which served *alcohol*. In my dealings with the motel, I'd long ago come to the point that I hated booze. Every time I saw a beer can, I saw Satan in it, with a big smile on his face. Until I began running The Longvue as a mission, I'd never seen the sheer destruction that alcohol can bring about. Only after witnessing so many lives destroyed because of it, and the overwhelming pain it often inflicts, did I really know what I was dealing with. And here I'm selling it myself, by way of The Peddler, when I'd just pleaded with a broken man to stop drinking—hypocrite!

That night in the motel parking lot, I just kept on walking, right across the street and into The Peddler. Just inside the front door, there stood Murray Broome, and I asked him then and there: "Would you like to buy me out?" His response was, "You won't believe it, Dipper, but yes, I would." Two things had just happened, I learned: first, Murray had decided against our longtime plan to sell The Peddler and then enter the real-estate business; and second, Murray's father had just retired and was now looking for investments, which had prompted the man to ask if Dipper might be interested in selling his share of the restaurant. Well, by the end of the week, I was, at long last, totally out of the restaurant business—and no longer a hypocrite! I did, however, keep my eating rights at The Peddler. I might not want any alcohol, but there was nothing wrong with their steaks!

* * *

Before leaving the subject of The Longvue, I should mention its most unlikely resident: my father-in-law, Burt.

His living there was a matter of health and circumstance. Although having suffered a stroke a while back (around the time Charlotte had fled back to New Jersey), Burt had, for several years, managed to continue living in his house, on his own, albeit with the assistance of a caretaker. But when he came to need constant care, independent living was no longer feasible, so Burt moved down to Boone, to reside at The Longvue for the last two years I had it. The arrangement allowed him to live by himself, as he wanted, while still being near enough for Charlotte to personally care for him. When Charlotte and I proposed one of The Longvue's three apartments, Burt agreed, even though he still didn't like me much.

Though Burt's two years at The Longvue could've gone better, the arrangement was functional enough. Charlotte started holding a Bible study in his apartment, with all the motel's womenfolk in attendance; but Burt never took interest. We knew that he'd never become a Christian, even after all those years of living with Charlotte's good Christian mother, Pearl (just like *my* dad, never taking up his wife's faith). But, as always, God had a plan, one which made all the trials and tribulations of the motel business worthwhile.

Yes, God was at work with old Burt.

Charlotte's women-only Bible study was instrumental in Burt's conversion. For him, religion was a bit of a sore topic. During the Bible studies, he would pretend not to hear, bowing his head over and lowering his hat like he was asleep. But he *did* hear, and we soon had ourselves a Christian Burt. Remember, the Bible tells us that God's word will not come

102

back void, and will always succeed. The lesson here: don't ever go by sight only, for you never know how God is working! If there was ever a hard case for winning to the Lord at the motel, it was, ironically, Charlotte's dad. Looking back, I have no doubt that, right from the beginning, this was one of the main reasons God had me take back The Longvue that last time—to answer Pearl's and Charlotte's prayers for Burt!

Coincidentally, it all worked out that just after Burt got saved, The Longvue was sold and, eventually, bulldozed down—as if it had finally fulfilled its purpose and was being laid to rest. (It was a miracle that the place had stayed up as long as it did.)

* * *

And that brings us to the second stage of my life in the motel business: The Elk.

After selling The Longvue, I owned The Elk motel for seven years total. I ran it, also, more as a mission than a business, aiming toward breaking even rather than turning a profit. Likewise, The Elk's story was The Longvue all over again: troubled people, rowdy behavior, Tony the conspiring-but-capable manager. Also like The Longvue, I struggled with it from the start, but it was all worth it, if only for those few lives that were changed there. And that's how it all stayed—until I got a letter one day, years after buying the place. Then, everything changed.

The letter in question was from the Boone health department, and the news wasn't good: the town was concerned about The Elk's septic system. You see, the motel was on a self-contained, field-style system (a large version of that used for a rural home), being about a quarter mile too far out for the city septic. According to the town, The Elk's field was overburdened and, therefore, overflowing onto the adjacent property—a big problem. As for the cause, it was no mystery: the septic system was old and inefficient to begin with, but then it was being further stressed by the motel's residents, who weren't too conservative with water usage (their utilities were included in their rent, removing any incentive toward responsible usage). To make matters worse, most of the residents lacked cars, and so they made use of the onsite laundry rather than the local Laundromat. The laundry was a mistake on my part, for it had begun when a lady discovered The Elk's washer and dryer, then asked if she could use them. Ignoring my better sense, I let my heart reply, telling her yes—after which, naturally, just about the whole motel was doing their wash there. After a couple years of laundry (on top of the high sewage load to be expected of any motel), the drainage problem arose.

This predicament was not easily solved, and it threatened the entire motel. Once I received the town's plaintive letter, I removed the onsite laundry, plus installed a meter so I could monitor water usage, but to little

103

effect. The ideal remedy would've been to extend the sewage field to accommodate more waste, but I hadn't the land to do so. The second-best solution—to convince the residents to significantly lower their water usage— was, unfortunately, no solution at all. I pleaded with them to cut down, asking that they run showers instead of baths, and to only flush the toilet when absolutely necessary (and to stop doing their laundry in the bathtubs, as had become the trend after I removed the laundry facilities)— but without results. Water usage stayed high, and I was left with one final option: to get the town to extend the city sewer out across that final quarter-mile between The Elk and Boone, so that the motel would no longer use its inadequate septic system at all. But, like the other two options, this one was not to be.

Admittedly, my request to run the sewer to the motel was a big one; then again, the expansion would have benefited others in the area, too (and would need to be done eventually, anyway, with the town growing in that direction). I begged town officials. I called every political connection I had. I gathered all the friends and acquaintances I'd amassed in my decades in Boone. I went so far as to mount a full-out "Save The Elk" campaign, which won support from townsfolk and the local press but not the local government. Everyone I talked to said the town wanted to help but couldn't, citing the gigantic bill that extending the city sewer even a quarter mile would entail. Also, there were other forces at work, powerful elements that were unsympathetic to the type of people the motel attracted, and wanted to spruce the town's image. Say what you will about those motives, but in any case, I was without a fix.

When all was said and done, the sewage problem would be The Elk's death knell, as well as that for my 25 years of ministering to the area's down-and-outs. My solution to the sewage problem was, eventually, to sell the property outright. The buyers converted the motel into student housing, and, ironically, the sewage problem was then solved, for the new tenants were not so liberal in their water usage. Under the lessened load, the septic field eventually dried out, and has been fine ever since. If only the motel residents would have been so conscientious.

But, really, the motel's closure wasn't such a bad thing, for I had long ago been exhausted by the operation. I think the Good Lord just knew I was worn out, and that it was time to bring my motel ministry to an end. There's a season for everything, and this season was over! My only regret in closing the motels is that it put a greater load on the area's other homeless ministries.

Anyway, I'll always be grateful for the opportunity the motels granted me to share the love of Christ!

Chapter XVII: A Great Toll Taken

As it turned out, the Lord was ready to end not only my motel ministry, but my being in the housing business altogether.

The sale of The Elk did not mean I was no longer a landlord—not by a long shot. By the time the sewage problem forced me to sell, I had a total of 36 other rental properties (and that wasn't counting those I'd unloaded already). These were all gifts from God, to be sure, but they were a lot of work, and I was tired (and not getting any younger). So when The Elk went, I just kept on selling out. It was how the Lord got me to shed the burden I'd been carrying, I think.

This, too, was a bittersweet affair. Yes, I was aging and tired, but I did hate to shutdown my rental empire, if only because I helped people through it much like the motels. I wanted to do all I could for the Lord, and reaching out through my rentals was a big part of that, but things were changing, as they always do, and I just had to go with it. Yes, the Lord had provided me the strength and desire to continue my ministry work for many years—but at great cost to myself and my family! You see, I didn't have a big crew of people working for me as I sat behind a desk and gave orders; I was the one doing the brunt of the work, right down to the physical labor (including that of *building* several of my rentals, pounding in each nail and carrying the masonry blocks and putting on roofs, and everything else). All this, while also moving houses, and ministering to the people in my motels and rentals and buildings (yes, I had whole apartment buildings, too), plus taking care of my family, and handling taxes and legal matters, and doing all the day-to-day stuff that life on earth requires of anyone—talk about stress! I'd been busy, and for a long time! To those who've known me throughout all this, they can testify that it is absolutely impossible for one person alone to do all that I did, that there's not enough time in the day—it was truly supernatural, accomplished only by the power of God. But, as I said, there's a season for everything, and the season for my crazy, overworked lifestyle was ending.

If there was anyone who understood why I was selling out and slowing down on work, it was Charlotte. When I gave her the news, she didn't have to be told why, being a firsthand witness to my life's craziness. She herself had given up a great deal in order for me to live and work like I did, and in recent years I'd been promising her I would slow down and give her more of my time, which she deserved. One thing I did for her was give her a second dream house, this one a vacation property in none other than Myrtle Beach, SC. Also, I built us a new home in Boone, which I called "the dump house," because most of the building materials had been recovered from the trash—everything except the plumping, electrical wiring, nails, and insulation! The house was constructed from all manner of odds and ends, including a chicken coop I'd torn down years prior, and even some things from The Longvue Motel. It had a cupola, too, which had, ironically, been scavenged from the town's original Holiday Inn before it was torn down for a new building (that which would occupy the old Longvue property). The amazing thing is that, for all the home's unusual construction, my wife loves it! The place took me about five years to build, and it's definitely one of a kind! By looking at it, you would never know its "ragtag" origins.

So, I'd sold out and my wife was happy, and when it came down to it, all those other reasons were secondary, for Charlotte herself was the biggest catalyst in this change. Specifically, it started in 2010, when she went to the hospital for a minor operation. The operation itself went fine, but two weeks afterward, she contracted C-Diff, one of those nasty bacterial infections that hospitals seem to attract. Charlotte was provided medicine, but the infection did not subside. Eventually, the doctor called me to his office, and I was told that he was unable to stop the C-Diff. Suddenly, there was question of Charlotte's survival!

In disbelief, I thought: *After all we've gone through, I'm going to lose her to some dumb little germ?!* However, I kept strong in my faith. As the Bible tells us in Romans 8:28, all things work for the good of those who love the Lord. Still, when I finished talking to the doctor and then went to see Charlotte, it was with a heavy heart. I kept remembering the pain of losing my mother. It all put things a little more in perspective, and that day in the hospital, I made a deal with the Lord: heal my wife, and I'll sell off the properties that were keeping me from devoting more time to her. I meant every word of it, despite the work it would entail.

It took three long months of battling the C-Diff infection, but Charlotte did, at long last, overcome it.

Afterward, I held to my end of the bargain. The very next day after hearing the good news, I began the years-long process of unloading my burdensome rental properties, which is ongoing to this day. So far, I've sold off the vast majority of my holdings, going from 36 various rentals to a half-dozen houses. What a difference! Now, I have a happy and healthy wife who gets to see her husband on a regular basis—maybe more than she wants to (she can't get rid of me). Plus, we can now spend more time at our dream house in Myrtle Beach, SC, another great blessing!

Chapter XVIII: Another "Only God" Story

Being so close to my heart, Myrtle Beach deserves its own chapter—especially the story behind my and Charlotte's house there (and *of course* there's a story behind it!).

Next to Boone, Myrtle Beach is our favorite spot. Charlotte loves restaurants, and the city by the sea has hundreds to choose from. It's such a beautiful place. In our many visits through the years, we had always stayed at a good, old motel in North Myrtle Beach (where our Peddler had been, so long ago), yet we had always dreamed of buying a beach home. We would always be checking out what was available on the market down there, but a suitable home evaded us. Our search went on year after year, and we nearly gave up, thinking there was no home with our name on it. But then we would remember that nothing is too difficult for God (which we of all people should know!).

Eventually, in fall of 2005, something happened to add some urgency to our search: the old North Myrtle Beach motel we frequented was being torn down. I like old motels, having owned two; unfortunately, those at the beach were being replaced by lucrative resorts and high-rises. Now, we were not only without a vacation home, but even our regular lodgings! So, while Charlotte and I were staying at the place for the last time (demolition was to begin literally the day after our checkout), we were really looking hard to find a vacation home before we left. Of course, God was right on time, for on the day prior to our departure, Charlotte saw a classified ad for a home for sale in an RV park, right in North Myrtle Beach. The park, a small gated community alongside a majestic marsh, was a little out of the way, in an area that we'd never visited in all our years of holidaying in the city, but we were getting desperate, so off we went to see the park home.

In the end, we did not buy the home in question; Charlotte didn't care for it. The park, however, she liked, so we asked the realtor if he knew of any other places there for sale (preferably on the marsh). The man said no, then left us in the park, having another appointment. "You're free to look around, if you'd like," the realtor told us before driving off. Figuring it couldn't hurt to look, we took the realtor's advice and drove around the RV park. Exploring, we soon came to a string of properties on the other side of the park, facing the marsh, and all sported a great view not only of the marsh, but the beautiful blue Atlantic! The spot was beyond our wildest dreams, and it was there that my wife noticed a quaint doublewide with a big yellow front door, pointing this one out in particular and saying how much she liked it. In fact, Charlotte was so enamored with this interesting home, we went looking for someone to talk to about it.

The first person we saw was an older woman, standing down the way from the yellow-doored place. I asked her if she knew anything about the house we were eying, and told her, "It's worth a thousand dollars to you," as an incentive. "Oh," the woman said then, memory lighting her face, "I think the one with the yellow door is for sale!" She didn't have the owner's contact information, but we did eventually find a sign with a phone number. This excited Charlotte, and her excitement only grew when we rounded the home and saw the incredible view from its back yard (a 180-degree panorama of the marsh and, beyond it, the Atlantic).

Our initial attempts at pursuing the yellow-doored home were unpromising. We tried calling the owner, but only got a machine. We left a message, but the afternoon passed without a call back. Our excitement waned. My wife wanted this place with all her heart, and remember, we were leaving Myrtle Beach the very next day. Out of desperation, we tried calling the phone number one more time, literally as we were walking out the door of the soon-to-be-demolished motel—and this time we got an answer! I talked to the owner, and we made arrangements to meet at the park home in an hour. Can you see God's hand in this?

By the time we got to the property, Charlotte was too excited to wait for the owner to show us around; the door was unlocked, so we went on in. The owner arrived soon after, and once we'd received a tour of the interior (which had my wife's name all over it, sporting all her favorite colors), Charlotte looked at me and said, "I want it! I want it!" Her excitement was so bad, I had to send her out to the car so I could negotiate a deal (have you ever tried dealing with someone who knows you want what they have?!). While out in the car, my wife prayed for the negotiations commencing in the house, and it would seem that her prayers worked. When all was said and done, the owner wanted $50,000 more than I was willing to pay, and we'd come to a stalemate—but then, miraculously, the owner came down another $40,000. This resuscitated the negotiations, and because I love my wife so much, and she loved the place so much, and we'd been looking for so long, I coughed up the extra $10,000. We had the papers drawn up that very day, and before that visit to Myrtle Beach was over, another dream had come true!

And, indeed, it was a dream come true, for the house proved every bit as wonderful as we'd imagined; truly, God does give us the desires of our hearts. After the sale, we found that we had not only a great house with a great view, but that the property was the highest spot on the South Carolina coast, being 28.5 feet above sea level. The property was so great, I can honestly say that I wouldn't trade it for anywhere else on the whole Atlantic seaboard, from Maine to Florida. The view really takes your breath away—only God could bring about such a deal! The beach house has been our little getaway for several years now. It's the perfect place, and a great blessing to my whole family. Charlotte gets so excited every time I tell her we're going there, and she cries when it comes time to leave—every time! That's how much Myrtle Beach means to Charlotte. The house, I think, was God's gift to her after all those years of toil and sacrifice that allowed me to minister to others—and oh! what a gift it was. We are forever grateful for it.

Chapter XIX: Finally Caught Up On My Mail

At this point in my life, having nearly died several times, built up (then sold off) multiple business empires, and run two motels as outreach missions, I was in my 60s, and more than ready for things to slow down.

Thankfully, they did, with no disastrous phone calls to foil my plans. I'd sold off most of my properties, and I was still selling more. Charlotte and I had our beach home. Our children were grown. One of the first things I did with my newfound time was to catch up on my mail, which I was about two years behind on. (In doing so, I discovered a check from an insurance company for $1,000. It had expired after 90 days, but I was able to get it reissued.) From there, I had a whole list of other things to catch up on, and I'm still working on them—life is an uphill battle, even in my semiretirement. Like so many others before me, I've discovered that it isn't easy getting old. Have you ever noticed how things change with age? I can remember my parents having a hard time getting me to go to bed; now I can't wait. Earlier in life you tend to think, *If I can just get through this, everything will be okay*—until, after enough living, you know that there will just be some other problem to take its place. And it just keeps right on going. It's always something!

By the time I'd sold out and settled down somewhat, I wasn't a young man anymore, and I knew it. Were my life a ballgame, I was in the final few minutes—which is to say, I wanted to make the most of my remaining time (I was a grandfather, after all, three times over). So I continued lessening my load. This extended even to my ministry. Charlotte and I do still spread the Gospel to others, and regularly pray for their salvation (we would love to see revival come to America before we finally pass on to our Heavenly home!), but just not to the frantic degree of times past. There is, however, one ministry I'll never stop: the corner.

Every week, I stand on a certain, prominent street corner in Boone, wearing a signboard proclaiming the Good News. It started way back in my motel days, almost 22 years ago, in 1994, when I wore a sign promoting a friend of mine who was seeking election as a judge. That particular corner would expose me to the most people, I reasoned, and so I walked it for a full two weeks, off and on. I can still remember the last day of that marathon sign campaign. It was a Friday evening and the election was on Tuesday, so I was thinking that I was about through, and that I couldn't wait to be done standing there! But I *wasn't* done: before I could leave the street corner that day, a still, small voice whispered in my ear, "Would you walk the corner for *Me?*" It was God, and my first thought was, *Oh no, Lord, anything but that. Send me to Africa, or China, but not the corner!* You see, it's a very humbling experience to stand on a corner wearing a great big signboard— you couldn't pay me enough to do it. But how could I say no to the Lord, after I'd long ago promised to do whatever He asked?

And so began my corner ministry. My brother, Raymon (who was by then living back in Boone, after many years in New Jersey), had a sign shop, and the week after God assigned me my task, I had a pair of signboards that proclaimed John 3:7 ("You must be born again") in attention-getting red-and-white type. Sure enough, I was back on the corner that weekend, now for the Lord rather than a politician. When I asked how long, He said, "Until I say stop." (*Or until I get run over,* I thought.) Well, He has yet to say stop (and I've yet to be run over, despite some close calls), so I can still be found on that corner, every Saturday. In addition to ministering to passing motorists, I'm able to do so with pedestrians on the sidewalk, too. To these, I've given out hundreds of tracts.

You can learn a lot from holding a sign on a corner. Passersby can be classified into three groups: 1) those who appreciate the message, and react with encouragement and excitement; 2) those who dislike the message, and react with offense; or 3) those who just don't care. Going on my years walking the corner, the two negative groups account for about 90% of my audience, leaving the minority to wave, honk their horns, or give me a thumbs-up. The majority, on the other hand, either pay no attention or react with all manner of ugliness. Shouted profanities, middle fingers, "I love Satan!," "I wish you were dead!"—you name it, I've probably gotten it on the corner. All because of a sign reading "Jesus Loves You." It really seems to anger many people, such that some have responded by driving right at the corner, making like they're going to hit me, only to steer away at the last moment. If I keep standing out there, it's only a matter of time before something happens to me; but I can't stop—and, really, I can't *lose.* If they run me over, I just go home to Heaven; if not, I go home to Charlotte!

Oh, I do have stories about the corner. For starters, those John 3:7 signs of mine. One day, in a hurry, I just threw the signs haphazardly into the back of my truck. Well, at some point they must've blown out, because when I got to where I was going, the signs were nowhere to be seen. I backtracked the road I'd been driving on but couldn't find the signs, so I ended up getting my brother's sign outfit to make up new ones. But, God used my loss to make lemonade out of lemons. A whole two years later, I was on the corner, doing my thing with the replacement signboards, when a man tapped me on the shoulder. "How long have you been standing out here?" he asked, to which I answered: "Several years." The man then told me how he'd been doing the same thing, over in Tennessee—because, one day while driving down the road, he'd come across some signboards printed with John 3:7, after which he'd picked them up and worn them on a corner over there! The man had found *my* lost signs, and put them to work— unbelievable! Another case of God's hand at work, now doing *double* duty!

Another time on the corner, I again got a tap on the shoulder, now from a man named Russell. He asked if he could stand with me, and I said sure. We made quite a pair, me being over 6'6", Russell being far shorter (and younger). He came back a few times, and eventually even had his own signs! Amazing! Shortly after, Russell moved to New Orleans, where he carried a sign on Bourbon Street. We corresponded every so often, and I learned that he later moved to San Francisco, where he continued the sign ministry. The last I heard from him, he was still out there, carrying his signs. God bless him and the Tennessean who'd found my signs, both!

When I'd obediently started my corner ministry, I really didn't know what God would do with it, or how. I was just to go out and witness for Christ, I thought—simple, you know? But it turned out to be more than that, for I've discovered, over the years, many other, unexpected results. For instance, my standing there not only got the Word out, but it *encouraged other Christians to get involved*, to themselves stand up and witness, like Russell and that other man. Once, a gentleman told me how his church had been trying to get him on a mission trip for years, but he'd always refused— until one freezing, windy day when he'd come upon me on the corner. "I thought," the man explained to me, "*If Dipper can stand on that corner in this kind of weather, I can go to South America on that mission trip.*" And so he'd finally accepted the church's mission assignment, and it had been the greatest experience of his life. "Thank you!" he finished. I've had many similar reports, thank God.

The corner works other kinds of miracles, too, of a more personal nature, and I'd like to share one of these in particular. One day while unloading trash at the county dump, I was approached by a little old lady. "Are you the fellow who stands on the corner?" she asked. I didn't know what to say; I'd once been attacked by someone who'd been offended by my message. But I told the truth, confirming that I was that fellow. The woman smiled then, and told me something that had happened to her a couple weeks prior. Feeling hopeless and that no one cared, she had decided to take her life, and meant it. But then she'd driven past me on the corner, and I'd turned around just as she saw me, so that she could read "Jesus Loves You" on my sign. "As soon as I read it, my life was changed," the woman said to me that day at the dump. Needless to say, she hadn't killed herself. Wow!

* * *

So, that's my corner ministry, which I plan to continue as long as I'm still vertical and breathing. If you ever hear that I was run over, don't feel bad, for I died being obedient to the Lord, and now I'm up in Heaven with Him!

Chapter XX: Of Faith and Fathers

Now, a word on the prime mover in my life's strange story: my faith.

If it's not yet clear, nothing gives me greater joy than sharing the gospel message with others so that they may receive the gift of salvation! I owe God everything, yet He owes me nothing, having "paid it all on the cross." He gave me salvation, and a personal relationship with Him. He saved me physically, too, many times over (and those are just the times I *know* of, never mind those I don't). He gave me two sons whom Charlotte and I love with all our hearts and are so thankful for! He gave me my little brother, too, and watched over him when I couldn't. And, of course, He saved my marriage, transforming my wife into a loving and devoted angel. Yes, the Lord provided for us, and took us through the dark times when things looked hopeless. He answered prayer after prayer over these many years, for which I can never thank Him enough. Yet, His greatest gift is still in the future: that one day Charlotte and I will see our moms and dads again, in Heaven.

What a wonderful God!

* * *

Speaking of dads.

The last I mentioned mine, he'd finally gotten over my mother's death, resumed his life, and married anew, to a wonderful woman named Eleanor. He continued living in New Jersey, and things were good. I was so grateful to see my dad have a life again, but once Charlotte and I came to the Lord, we had a great burden for him and my stepmother. They were good people, to be sure, but being good doesn't get you into Heaven. For several years Charlotte and I prayed for my folks, and witnessed to them personally when possible, but we didn't seem to be getting anywhere. Then, in 1990, my dad got cancer, and a door was opened.

The man was in his seventies by then, and it soon became clear that the cancer was terminal. Time was short, Charlotte and I knew, so we decided to take the kids up to Jersey for a week. It was a difficult trip, to say the least, for I knew it would be the last I saw my father. I had a heavy heart, but I was able to share my faith with him, and we had some good, meaningful conversations—but without fruit, for he remained an unbeliever. So, on our last day there, I poured my soul out to him, pleading that he accept the gift of salvation; but still to no avail. Defeated, I said my goodbyes and walked out to the car, where Charlotte was waiting with the boys. When I met her there, I said, "I don't know how I can leave. I have no assurance of my dad's salvation." Her look was the same as mine, and I decided then not to leave without some hope. So I went right back inside, walked over to my dad in his chair, and got down on my knees.

"This is probably the last time I'm ever going to see you," I told him. "I've spent the last seven days sharing my faith with you, and I know you've listened, but I still have no assurance you're going to accept Jesus as your savior. Time is running out, and I can't leave without some hope!" I then played my last remaining card: I asked my dad if he knew where my mother was. "Heaven, without a doubt," he answered at once. Next, I asked if he wanted to see her again, to which he responded: "With all my heart!" Finally, I proceeded to tell him that there was only one way that would happen: by accepting Christ as his savior.

"Son," my dad said then, "I won't lie to you and tell you something I don't believe. I need a little time to digest all we've talked about this week, and I promise you I'll do the right thing!" Tears down my face, I got up and said, "That gives me hope." I hugged him, kissed his cheek, and said goodbye for the last time. Back at the car, Charlotte had been praying. "Did he accept?" she asked when I emerged from the house. "No," I told her, "but I have some hope. We can leave, now."

Yes, I had hope, and it was not in vain.

Two weeks later, my dad was in the hospital, though they couldn't help him much. He was in great pain, and generally suffering from his cancer (I hate cancer; it's straight from the pit of Hell). I'd been praying 24/7 just about, not only for my dad but for Eleanor too. It was a dark time, but I relied on the promises of God, that I could trust Him and that He was at work! Then, while I was driving home for lunch one day, I heard His voice, as clear as could be: "Your dad is now ready. Call Jimmy and ask him to go see your dad at the hospital." Jimmy was the pastor of Charlotte's home church up in Jersey.

Upon hearing God's command, I put the pedal to the metal, breaking all speed limits to get home (this was before cellphones). Once there, I ran inside and told Charlotte to call Jimmy. Though it would be her first call to the man (they were not close), she didn't ask me why, just looked up his number, picked up the phone, and dialed, perhaps sensing the urgency. Jimmy answered on the second ring—although he was never home at that hour, as he later told us. That day, Jimmy had only been there because he'd promised his wife he would paint a room of their house, after having repeatedly put it off—what a "coincidence"! He'd been determined to get this job done, but upon being asked by Charlotte to go to the hospital and see my dad (whom Jimmy had never met), Jimmy agreed to go—a bit begrudgingly, having just changed into his painting clothes, but he went.

Later that day, Jimmy called back with good news: in less than fifteen minutes of Jimmy's arrival at the hospital, my dad and Eleanor had both accepted the gift of salvation, responding to Jimmy's presentation of the Gospel message. According to Jimmy, the pain left my dad's face upon his profession of faith, replaced by peace and comfort. After hearing the news, Charlotte and I praised the Good Lord for what He'd done! There are no words to express the joy and assurance that overcame us, and our gratitude to Jimmy for going to the hospital on such short notice—what an answered prayer!

Five weeks later, my dad passed away, at home, still wearing that peaceful expression.

* * *

Great as my parents' salvation was, the Lord still wasn't done yet, for He had more ministry work in store for Charlotte and I.

After my dad's passing, in 1990, we headed back up to Jersey, now for the funeral, which sent us on a truck route through the heart of Delaware. This road was just a narrow, two-lane highway with tractor-trailers going over 65 miles per hour—a pretty treacherous stretch of road, unfriendly to pedestrians. Yet, as Charlotte and I were riding it, that's just what we saw: a pedestrian. Worse, just as we noticed the man, he collapsed into the street!

We pulled over immediately, and I told Charlotte to run into a nearby convenience store and call an ambulance (again: no cellphones back then). Meanwhile, I jumped from the car and ran to the man lying in highway, pulling him to my chest just as a truck flew by—so close I could feel its tailwind on the backs of my hands! The man was unconscious, and while we waited for the ambulance together, I had a chance to pray for him. As the paramedics placed him in the ambulance and closed the doors, I happened to say "Jesus" out loud—and with that, the man regained consciousness, an enormous grin on his face! It was the last I saw of the fellow, but I'm sure the Lord took care of him.

Another of God's "divine appointments," for sure!

Also, there's a bit of a back story to the man's rescue from that perilous highway, and no small amount of irony. See, when my dad was 19 years old, he hit and killed a man on a bicycle. It was late at night, and my dad was driving down a rough, gravel, backwoods road—when he collided with something. Thinking it a deer, he stopped and got out, only to find that he'd run over a bicyclist. In addition to being a dark-skinned black man, the

119

victim was wearing a dark coat, and riding a dark-colored bike with no reflectors—my dad had never even seen him. My dad had been so upset about the accident, he wouldn't drive a car for the next two years. In that time, he walked just about everywhere he went.

So, isn't it ironic that on the way to my dad's funeral I would rescue a man (who was also black) from getting run over? It would seem that the Lord used my dad's death for something good, and I don't think anything could've made him happier! Plus, once I at last arrived at my dad's viewing, I was able to tell the story to the hundred-odd attendees, which was beneficial in its own right. There wasn't a dry eye in the room, and it seemed to help lift the funeral's depressing air, such that the service was almost joyful. Later, I was able to tell everyone how my dad had accepted the Lord, too, and the service became even more positive—which the Lord was also able to use.

I learned about this last part only afterward, when I was approached by a friend who'd been in attendance. He told me that there'd been a second service held at the funeral home at the same time as my dad's, and my friend had slipped over into it briefly. "Dipper," he told me then, "the difference was like night and day." My dad's service was predominantly Christian, with people celebrating that he'd gone on to Heaven, whereas the other service, my friend said, was "filled with darkness and despair." See, that man hadn't been a Christian, and his family had been without hope of ever seeing him again. According to my friend, those folks were instead arguing over who got what from the dead man's estate. "It changed my whole outlook on things," my friend finished, having been exposed to the comparative ugliness of the other service. Charlotte and I had prayed that God would bring something good of my dad's funeral, and my friend's new outlook certainly fit the bill!

With my dad buried, all four of my and Charlotte's parents were now with the Good Lord. My dad had gotten his wish to see my mom again, surely, just as my wife and I have our assurance that we'll be together for eternity. Once more, I can't praise God enough for all He's done (and continues to do)! Isn't He great?

Chapter XXI: Time

Because of all that I've been through, I would now like to discuss what I believe to be one of our most precious gifts from God: time.

I think that if you asked most older people what they most regret about their lives, their answer would involve how much time they've wasted! You've heard it repeatedly, how short our lives are; life is like a vapor, flying by before you know it. It's a real tragedy that most of us don't regard time in a serious way, but instead take it for granted, especially early in life. Yes, time truly is a gift, which really levels the playing field for all. Each of us gets exactly 24 hours a day, which doesn't ever change, and it's up to each person to decide what to do with their time, and how it will affect our entire life (and the lives of those around us). Each person will sleep away nearly a third of their life, and another third will be spent working, learning, and tending to our homes and families, while more still is allotted to things like food and leisure and caring for oneself (and, hopefully, helping others). It all comes down to this: we don't have a lot of time to lose, and this is why we must be mindful of how we make use of it every day. We will be held personally accountable for every decision we make, and for how we invest this gift of time. Time is so valuable, and so limited, we musn't neglect any of it. We either use it or lose it—the choice is ours!

You can't buy or create it—not one second—but you can, however, decide that you will utilize whatever time you have left. Realize the importance of planning how to use your time each day. Remember: we can't go back and change how we spent time in the past, but we can choose not to waste this great commodity in the future. Altogether, a balanced and well-invested life—one that makes the very most of each moment—will lead to fewer regrets when that life is at its close.

There are many different ways we can handle our time:

Stretch it
Protect it
Guard it

Control it
Cherish it
Sell it
Invest it
Honor it
Spend it
Use it
Ponder it
Give it
Waste it
Neglect it
Regret it
Lose it
Blow it

As for the most important moment of our time on this Earth, that would, ideally, be the one in which we receive the greatest gift of all: the Lord Jesus Christ! In those few seconds that you accept *that* gift, it is decided where you will spend your time in eternity. So, please, don't miss this opportunity. Respond now and receive the precious gift of salvation, and you'll never regret what you did at this time!

To receive this gift, just pray this simple prayer:

Dear Heavenly Father,

> *I come to You confessing that I have sinned and broken Your laws, and ask You to forgive me. I believe that Jesus Christ came to Earth to die for me and my sins on the cross, and that on the third day He rose from the dead, that I may have eternal life. I surrender my life to You and ask now for Your plan for my life. Thank You for the gift of salvation.*

> *I pray this prayer in Jesus' name. Amen!*

I praise God for your salvation, and encourage you to read the following Bible verses:

Romans 3:10 and 10:9-13
Acts 17:30
The Gospel of John

Chapter XXII: The End of the Story—For Now

And so we come to the end of my life's strange and winding story, in 2015.

I have many more tales I could tell, but I think I can sum up them all by saying that God has always been at work in my life. Like a great tailor, He has woven His plan throughout my affairs—there's just no other explanation. As I've written this book, I realize God's intricate planning only more plainly. This plan was not of my own making; it was much greater than I could have ever dreamed or imagined, and it was at work from day one. I didn't always enjoy it at the time, but in hindsight I can see that it was all for my own good, for God doesn't make mistakes.

It's best, I feel, to conclude this book with some observations, to share my life's accumulated knowledge somewhat.

First: time. Oh, time is a funny thing. It flies by so fast, a lot of my tales seem like they happened just yesterday! I'm so glad that I realized at an early age how valuable time is, so I could make the most of each minute, every day. I have no regrets about how I've spent my time in this world. A common regret I've heard from so many people is what they did with their time: how they'd wasted it, after realizing they only get one life, one chance. One bad decision can change a life forever, and one good one can do the opposite! So I say, don't waste your precious time.

Next observation: relationships. They are so important, and I have surely been blessed with some good ones, for their impact on me. I do regret the girl who claimed to love me, then traded me for a new car; but then, if she hadn't, I never would've met my angel, Charlotte, who gave me all her love and asked very little in return. Don't take relationships for granted. Treasure them, and realize what a true gift they are.

And speaking of gifts: know that we all have some gift that the Lord wants to use for His glory! We just have to find out what it is, then cultivate it. How many people go through life without ever discovering their gift or purpose? That's what, I believe, a lot of us are searching for (but in all the wrong places). That's why, when you *do* find your purpose, it results in such great happiness. Otherwise, we are left with the infamous "void," that feeling of emptiness in our hearts that we've all experienced. Let it be known: nothing can fill that void but God! So many of us try to fill it with so many other things—wealth, fame, accomplishment, love. But none of those substitutes will do, because God made it so that satisfaction results only from a relationship with Him!

Most people think money will bring fulfillment, I've learned over the years. But I can assure you, material wealth is not the answer. I've known many people who, despite very little money or possessions, were fully happy and content—and I've known millionaires who were the most miserable human beings you'll ever meet! There's a third category, too: those who try to fill the void with relationships. Yes, good relationships are important, but even the best will never replace the one with God Almighty.

Here's another hard-won tip of mine: live a healthy and well-balanced life. Abuse yourself with alcohol and drugs, and, trust me, you'll pay for it. You only get one body, and it's like a car: neglect it, and it won't keep going too long. Healthy living is so beneficial, in so many ways. I've never met anyone who regretted sobriety, good diet, and regular exercise. What you put in your body (and what you *don't*) can have bearing on everything in life, from education, to your spouse, job, and friends, even to whom or what you put your faith in. Truly, a healthy lifestyle plays a big part in what sort of life you live and what kind of person you become.

The same goes for work: you must love it. You can't spend your life doing something you hate without it taking a toll! Find a job you enjoy, and you'll be much more satisfied with life overall. From there, that enjoyment will extend outward, to a happy wife and kids, to your neighbors and acquaintances, all of which will increase your chances of a successful life. Be content with your occupation, and it can make all the difference in the world.

Marriage is another crucial part of a good life. After my marital issues with Charlotte, I know this better than anyone. A sound marriage will translate to a better life; and for a sound marriage, husband and wife must be on the same page, spiritually content in their relationship and willing to put one another first. Instead live in some make-believe fantasy, and this will affect everything else, too, usually to detrimental ends. That's why God says not to be unequally yoked. And, always remember: men are from Venus and women are from Mars (especially left-handed women, like Charlotte). Keeping this in mind will go a long way toward solving marital problems. (God made us so different, I believe, so that marriage would require His help!)

I hope these observations have shed a little light on this amazing thing we call life, and how to live it to the fullest. I would like to see others learn and apply things from my experience rather than have to learn them on their own, through "hard knocks." The earlier we learn the principles of good living, the better.

Well, I believe the Book of Dip has covered enough of my life (maybe more than you wanted to know). But that doesn't mean there isn't more to my story; this book is, in fact, just a taste of what the Lord has done in my life. Here, I feel like John when he ended his book in the Bible: if he wrote the *whole* story of God's greatness, there wouldn't be enough room in all the world.

If you'd told me, growing up, that this would be my life, I wouldn't have believed you—not even close! Where I go from here, only God knows, for He is my story's sole author! So, I close this book without knowing its end—and I believe it's better that way! All I know is that I trust God, and that I'll be obedient and make sure that His will be done. Until He chooses to at last conclude the long, complicated book of my life (what a trip it's been!), I'll keep doing His work—planting seeds, encouraging others, and "fighting the good fight." I know there will be more battles, but that's life, and I'll always praise and thank Him for all He's done.

And as for *you*, thanks for reading my story! I pray that God has used it to speak to you in some way. My one desire for you is the same that Dr. Davies (who "lost" my hospital bill after my motorcycle accident) had for me: to become a personal, living witness for Christ. Don't just "talk the talk"; *show* the world your faith, using words only when necessary.

In conclusion, I'll say that life is a battle, especially as a practicing Christian, for we fight not only the world of the flesh, but *Satan* too! But, we can never give up, and we must always remember our blessed hope in Jesus Christ. With this in mind, I leave you with a "hotline" number for the Lord, from Jeremiah 33:3: Call to Me, and I will answer you and show you great and mighty things which you do not know.

And my story continues on! May God bless you as He has me!

In God's Name,
Floyd "Dipper" Garrison
Boone, NC
2015

Coda

So, you thought I was finished—not just yet!

As a final footnote, I would now like to present an obituary I read recently. Obviously, I won't be around to read my *own* obituary, so I will, instead, put forth this one in its place, for posterity. This particular obituary, of a local woman who died at the grand age of 91, struck me as poignant, and also as a great, posthumous witness for Christ—just what I want mine to be!

I will quote it now, in part. Consider it applying to me, also.

[...] I have lived a full and wonderful life. My life story has been read by my friends and family for 91 years. It is now complete. I was blessed to have been loved by so many. My greatest blessing and privilege was to love others. The greatest gift I imparted to this world was my one and only very special daughter, [name]. The greatest gift I ever received was My Lord and Savior Jesus Christ. Do not cry for me. Laugh, smile, and remember! Love as I have loved. Live as I have lived, full of joy, compassion, love, mercy, and grace. Believe as I have believed in God's one and only Son. I wish to see you all again. I know I will if you heed these words. My love you will always have in your hearts. My life story you will always have in your thoughts and in your dreams. Do not mourn me for I live. Celebrate my new life. My greatest dream has come true. I am now content, happy, perfected, and whole. Thank you all! Thank you Christ Jesus my Lord! [...]

When my day comes, I hope to hear these words: "Well done, my good and faithful servant!" Amen.

Made in the USA
Columbia, SC
19 October 2020

23129937R00076